A Liar's
Autobiography

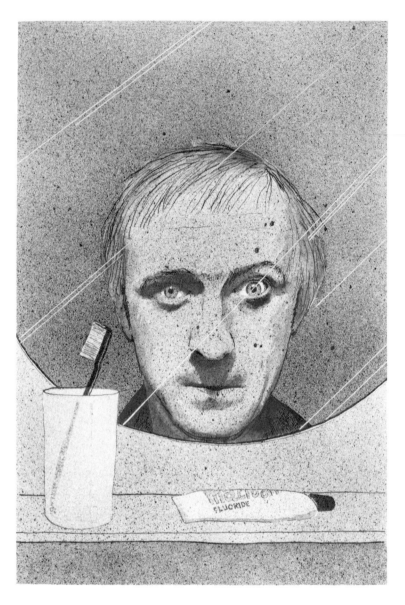

I was going to stick it out . . .

A Liar's Autobiography

VOLUME VII

by GRAHAM CHAPMAN

and David Sherlock
and also Alex Martin
Oh, and David Yallop
and also too by Douglas Adams
(whose autobiography it isn't)

with drawings by
Jonathan Hills

Eyre Methuen

First published in Great Britain in 1980
by Eyre Methuen Ltd, 11 New Fetter Lane,
London EC4 4EE
Reprinted 1980

Copyright © 1980 by Sea Goat Productions Ltd
ISBN 0 413 47570 0

Filmset, printed and bound in Great Britain by
Hazell Watson & Viney Ltd, Aylesbury, Bucks

Contents

About the Co-authors

For an autobiography this book has an unusual number of authors, some of whom I should like to thank for their impatience. In particular:

DAVID A. YALLOP. One of the non-existent co-authors of this autobiography; has written several books on his own including *To Encourage the Others* and *The Day the Laughter stopped*. There was another co-author but he was murdered in a dispute over copyright. M. Yallop demeure maintenant en Nouvelle Zélande.

DOUGLAS N. ADAMS. An author not previously mentioned by name, had not in fact been murdered and was merely playing possum under a pile of previously unpublishable scripts (see *Hitch-Hiker's Guide To The Galaxy*). He will probably be shoving a few words in here and there over the next few dozen pages, but only admits this fairly hesitantly because though David A. Yallop is not 6' 5", he is extremely fierce.

ALEX MARTIN. Born in 1953 in Baltimore, 'the armpit of America', or was it Wisconsin, 'the crotch of the world'; lasted longer than any of the other co-authors with the exception of David Sherlock who proves the rule.

Educated at Winchester College and Cambridge University, this one-time co-authorship longevity record-holder still has my considerable esteem.

PEDRO MONTT. An ex-Chilean president who, with his conservative government, preferred to advance railroads and manufacturing industries and to ignore pressing social and labour problems rather than write other people's autobiographies.

DAVID J. SHERLOCK. A debonair young pouff-about-town who was born on the Welsh border in 1947. Luckily things have improved and he is now pretty hot property in the harsh masculine world of book publishing. He has remained a close personal friend for the last 14 years officer.

On Lying and the Brave Men who do it

It is a curiosity of post-Boer War European literature (and I firmly include Great Britain in the term 'European') that prefaces beginning 'It is a curiosity' hardly ever have anything to say. In fact I've become so convinced of this rule that whenever I see those four grovelling words at the start of a book I shut the damn thing at once and throw it on the fire. What, you will ask, does one read instead? Well there's one book I turn to time and again. *A Liar's Autobiography* by Graham Chapman, David Sherlock, Alex Martin, Douglas Adams, and David Yallop. It doesn't have much to say, but at least it doesn't start 'It is a curiosity', and that's good enough for me.

Captain Mark Phillips
(no letters after my name, but
I am fairly rich)

On Lying and the Brave Men who do it

Now that you're over that first fence, which my husband wrote for money, I'd like to try to sketch out some of the tricky jumps ahead of anyone who really wants to score points on this notorious epistemological event. Let's start with the first obstacle, a very deceptive one where you can land on your b . . . . m (I'm not allowed to put 'bottom') unless you concentrate absolutely one hundred per cent. 'All men are liars,' said Charles. Now think carefully. What does this imply? It implies that Charles is a liar himself, so if he's telling the truth he's actually lying, and if he's lying he's telling the truth. Do you see what I'm driving at? It's a jolly tricky one, that. The next obstacle is also jolly tricky. It looks like one of those children's riddles, and in fact that's just what it is – rather mean I think, especially so early in the round! But here it is anyway: you're riding along a country lane when suddenly you come to a fork in the road. You see a sign saying, 'One of these roads leads to Newmarket, the other to somewhere horrid.' To find out which is which, you have to ask one of the two brothers who live in the hut over there. But there's the catch. One of them only tells the truth, and the other tells only lies. And you can only ask one question. Think carefully before you ask!

Well, that really is tricky, isn't it? I'm afraid I can't give you any help on that one, as I've forgotten the answer myself, but anyway, good luck, and rest assured that even though I can't be bothered to tell you any more about lying I am actually quite good at it.

Mrs Captain Mark Phillips

'Heads which are empty and
weak are always liable to
get little black things
inside which rattle about.'

E. W. Shepherd-Walwyn
Look Straight Ahead:
Twenty Talks with Boys and
Boy Scouts

CHAPTER NOUGHT

11 a.m. 26th December 1977

I was going to stick it out, and do it cold this time. No drugs to alleviate the symptoms of withdrawal. I had spent a sleepless night, sweating and shivering. Maybe I had slept and was now dreaming that I hadn't slept, in which case I must be asleep. I turned over, thumped the pillow into shape, and tried to relax. My toes and shins were numb. I tried to check for sensation, first with one foot against the other, then with trembling hands. The harder I tried to steady my hands the more uncontrollable they became.

You'll be all right if you just stay in bed. You don't have to do anything today, you don't have to see anybody, talk to anybody, eat anything, or drink anything. Just stay in bed and see it through.

It didn't matter if I hadn't slept all night, I could sleep all day, and even if I couldn't sleep today I could spend a whole week in bed if necessary. That's what I'd do. I felt better, sat up. I reached out for my pipe, picked it up from the ashtray. That was good. I was doing well. I picked up a box of matches, opened it – my hands were only shaking slightly. I lit my pipe, shook the match to put it out, tried to blow it out, dropped my pipe, threw the match into the ashtray and watched it burn out. I picked up my pipe, tried to put it in the ashtray, and missed by a couple of inches, knocking the ashtray onto the floor. Forget about the pipe and the ashtray. Nothing's burning. Leave them.

I relaxed back onto my pillow but dodged suddenly as an anglepoise lamp prepared to attack me . . . but then didn't. It stayed where it was. The terrible itching started again. I remembered now – that was what had been keeping me awake. There were insects all over me.

In the hall outside I could still hear the clock; the soft, comforting, regular 'tock'. There was no 'tick', the clock was just saying 'tock'. I listened hard for the 'tick'. It wasn't there and of course I knew why. I had become so infuriated at the regularity of its thumping message – not 'tick-tock' but 'breeze-block, breeze-block, breeze-block' (I had even tried to change it to 'tea-pot, tea-pot') – that I had carried the clock into another room, covered it with pillows, and gone back to bed, closing both doors. That was why I could only hear the soft, distant 'tock . . . tock . . . tock . . . tock . . . tick-tock . . . tick? . . . tock . . . tick-tock . . . breeze-block, breeze-block' – Oh Christ, leave me alone . . . I buried my head in the pillows. I could hear nothing. I listened hard. Nothing . . . except the distant 'breeze-block, breeze-block'. I sat up. The bedroom door was open. The clock was still on the landing. I remembered bumping into it as I lurched past it, after throwing up the last time. And the pillows – they were still on the bed. It must have been a dream. So I *had* slept. Right then – I'll get up and go downstairs and just spend the rest of the day watching television. There's going to be no-one around except John, David and Batch. They've all seen me with the shakes before, and I've told everyone that I'll be away for Christmas. . . .

When you're not sure whether you're going to throw up or not the last thing you need is someone fussing – 'Are you all right? You look a bit pale. Would you like a nice cup of tea? And perhaps a thin slice of toast with a poached egg on top?'

I was about to make the decision to get out of bed when David came in and asked me how I was, and was there anything I wanted, like a nice . . .

'No,' I snapped. But the words for the rest of the sentence, although formed in my head, just wouldn't articulate themselves. 'I'm . . . I'll . . . j-j-j-j-just leave . . . mo . . . mm . . . ment. Later p-p-per . . . get up be fine. . . .'

'Vichy water?'

'No . . . y-y-yes!'

He plumped up the duvet. I flinched. It was out to get me, in league with the clock, and the tablelamp, the pipe, the ashtray, the matches.

'You just stay there,' he said, and very sensibly left the room.

'D-D-David . . . curtains . . . l-l-light.' The curtains were still drawn, but there was a chink at the top through which a laser beam from the world outside was threatening me. . . .

Oh fuck all this – you'll be all right. Pull yourself together, man. Get dressed.

I threw off the stifling duvet and sat up with my feet on the floor. I slowly dressed, clutching on to anything I could find for support, lurching around the room. I drew the curtains and felt better – nothing in the room was moving except for me. I picked up my pipe and lit it. This simple, for me automatic, action gave me confidence. I composed myself. Usually about half an hour after getting up in the morning if I hadn't managed to down at least five measures of gin there would be the coughing fit accompanied by the dry heaves, the coughing, the cold sweat, and uncontrollable shivering. But it was 11.30, perhaps I had stayed in bed long enough to miss out this daily genuflection and regurgitative prayer over the lavatory bowl.

The bedroom doorpost took a swipe at me as I walked past: a mild hallucination. I steadied myself for my walk down the stairs – stairs which I knew either stopped before I finished going down them, or carried on after I had stopped, with banisters that were never quite in the same place, cornerposts that made sudden lunges at me, hoping that I would lose concentration and bang my head on shadows. But I was too quick for the shadows and ducked, only to walk straight into a right-hand uppercut from the cornerpost which had got round me with its clever footwork. Back to bed.

Forty-four hours of febrile paranoia and auditory and tactile hallucinations followed in that restless bed. Sheer exhaustion won, and I slept for a few hours, and I knew that I had this time. I'd sweated it out. The worst was over. Even the stairs had suspended hostilities. I managed to drink a cup of tea, keep down some vitamin pills *and* a slice of toast with a poached egg on it. I was free. I went into the dining-room, quite calmly walked past three shelves of Christmas booze and rang Bernard and Jane, my secretary, to ask them round for a drink – provided, I added smugly, they could stand the sight of me drinking tonic water.

They came round to the house. I poured them a drink, while apologizing for slightly trembling hands. They were both pleased that I had recovered so quickly, and as I poured myself a neat slimline tonic, I explained to them how much more confident I was of staying off alcohol for good now that I'd done it the hard way. As I picked up my drink I knocked over a Christmas card. I put my glass down and tried to stand the Christmas card up again. My fingers wouldn't keep still. 'Don't bother about that,' said Bernard. 'Sit down.'

I was bothered about it. It was the only thing that mattered. I had to stand that Christmas card up. The harder I tried, the worse I shook.

'I'm all . . . ri . . . ght.' The shaking was now a rhythmic shuddering which turned into a sudden spasm and I fell to the ground, taking with me a pile of glasses, bottles and Bernard.

I woke up to flashing blue lights. There was an ambulance outside. What was that doing here? I felt fine, and I'd had worse cuts. Everyone persuaded me that perhaps hospital was the best thing. Jane was gaping as though she'd just been witness to an exorcism. I was carried off to the hospital, knowing that I'd lost my heroic struggle with the distilleries of the world. Perhaps two bottles of gin a day was hitting the stuff a bit hard. Bernard later pointed out to me that over the last six months, because I'd been buying in bulk, I had moved on to the pub size bottles, that is forty fluid ounces each, making an average daily consumption of four pints imperial

(2 ½ US quarts). It was enough to preserve a cadaver – or kill six Encratites.

St Alvar's Hospital probably has some well-equipped and modern wards, and parts of it may well be the very best in the land, but I was taken to none of these bits. I was destined for the National-Health-as-it-really-is parts of the edifice of healing – dingy corridors, overcrowded wards, underworked staff, Hogarthian inmates, Boadicean plumbing and a television that you had to pedal.

Quantities of blood were taken for analysis, I was pumped full of vitamins, and drugged up to my toupee with heminevrin and valium. But the Rasputin in me cut through the fog of sedation like a bottle of Cutty Sark. I knew that I was not living in the style to which I had become accustomed, and decided that those who could pay for medicine should. I was taken to a private clinic in which there was luckily one Arab-free bed. My personal physician and hard-drinking companion, his Efficaciousness A. R. Bailey the Practical, M.R.C.P., brought along a remarkably sane psychiatrist whose name, for the purposes of this book, I shall give in the form of a *Times* crossword clue:

ACROSS
1. Familiar French horseman on the tip of one's tongue ruins musical pedigree. (7, 8).

Dr One Across, having known me since medical school, gave analytical flummery the elbow, and said, 'Graham, you're an alcoholic.'

I said, 'Yes.'

He said, 'D'you want not to be?'

I said, 'Yes.'

He said, 'Right. We'll start the treatment. Your liver function tests were appalling, ten times over the acceptable norm for the Gamma GTP, for instance. But there's no sign of enlargement, and with a bit of luck there's a chance that you may not have damaged your liver permanently. We'll phase out the heminevrin and valium gradually, and you can take one Abstem tablet in the morning and one in the evening, so that if you do drink any alcohol you will feel as ill as you were five days ago. It's up to you whether you drink or not. It's your liver. It's your life. . . .'

Dr One Across left me valiumed up a treat along with the children, whose little faces shone with anticipation as in came Puss followed by Dick Whittington. 'Oh dear Puss,' said Dick. 'London is far behind us, what shall we do now?'

'Miaow!'

'What's that? Sing a song?'

'Miaow!'

'What, now, for all the children?'

'Miaow!'

'Shall we sing a song, children?'

'Yes!'

The words were lowered from the ceiling, and as the band struck up 'The March of the Liberty Belle' we all joined in the song:

> 'Of all the organs the body contains
> The liver's the one for me:
> It processes food, it deals with the waste,
> It's cleverer than a knee.
> When it throws up its hands at alcohol,
> And makes you extremely ill,
> It's best to take heed, you're not being a weed,
> You're just being sensibil.'

'Dizzy Gillespie wrote that,' I said.

'He may have done, but Fenchurch Street Station is mine, so, Jane, that's £150 you owe me,' said Bernard.

'You've only got two stations,' said Jane.

'I bought Marylebone from you last time you landed on Graham's hotel on Old Kent Road.'

'Oh well that's me out, then.'

'No it isn't. There's still plenty of property you can mortgage.'

'I'm not going to mortgage those. I'm going to build there.'

'You haven't got the money.'

'All right, I'll give you the waterworks.'

'I don't want it. Perhaps Graham does.'

'Graham, d'you want the waterworks? . . . Graham?'

'No, I'll buy the camelopard.'

'What?'

'It's a camel that looks like a leopard. A giraffe.'

'He's gone again,' said Bernard.

A pantomime . . . Dizzy Gillespie . . . camelopard . . . I was clearly making a good recovery. Even without alcohol I was thinking irrationally, and generally being an odd sort of fellow don't you know. What ho, old chap, how's the gazebo?

Do you know, last time I was in Paris I really did ring Jean-Paul Sartre and Simone de Beauvoir answered the phone and said that he was out distributing leaflets. Or was that a sketch?

Leaving that side of my mind to play around with itself for a while, the rest of it brought itself up to date.

I was feeling good. My self-imposed treatment was over. With the use of alcohol I had managed to kill exactly the number of brain cells I had decided to lose at the age of twenty-two, without sacrificing my liver.

There's no doubt that an excess of alcohol accelerates the death of brain cells, and that in small doses, as with any other anaesthetic, it can temporarily put them out of action, starting at the top and working down the central nervous system. It's the inhibitory influences of the higher centres of the brain which are the first affected. That's why alcohol is so commonly used as an aid to social intercourse. It can help you say 'Hello' to new friends; 'Goodbye' to old friends; 'D'you want to come back to my place?' to strangers, or 'Why don't you fuck off?' to tediosities. If you're onto a cert, the last thing you need is something nagging away at the front of the brain saying, 'Perhaps another time . . . with someone else . . . anyway . . . might laugh at my willie'. What you need is another pint.

To cure my own inhibitions, however, I had discovered a long time ago that another pint and then another was not enough. I was interested in something more permanent. I needed to rid myself of my cramping fetters for ever. I had prescribed an extensive course of heavy drinking, in order to actually kill off all offending nerve cells – a hazardous treatment, in that some of the more useful cells, those responsible for keeping oneself within the limits of socially acceptable behaviour, also received a heavy battering.

So what could have been the story of a kind-hearted, respectable medical practitioner, isn't.

CHAPTER ONE

Perinatal Development and a Few Other Bits

I was born in Leamington, now officially known as Royal Leamington Spa, moderately famous for the manufacture of gas cookers (see Chapter 14), about which more anon[1]. The year was 1942, and the period of gestation ended on the seventh of February during a rather botched-up air raid in which the Germans thought they were hitting Coventry – but more of that anon[1], which is a word I'm very fond of[2]. My parents, Tim and Beryl, sorry, Tim and Betty[3],

1. A very stupid word which won't be used again in this book.
2. None of this is true. (I was in fact born in Stalbridge in Dorset but if you want to send any letters there please note that the correct postal address is Stalbridge, STURMINSTER NEWTON, Dorset). The correct date of birth was Jan 6th 1940.[4]   3. Actually Walter, Edith and Mark.
4. Complete rubbish. I was not born in Dorset. My current co-author had lived in Stalbridge for several years which is how it crept in. I think he's getting a bit fed-up with this book being all about me. This is going to be a bit difficult to control as he's actually writing it out[5].
5. Bloody hell. This is far too complicated. Can't we just leave this and say, 'see *About the Co-authors*?' (Alex)[6].   6. 'Yes, that's fine.' (David).

were outraged when I arrived because they'd been expecting a heterosexual, black Jew with several rather amusing birth deformities as they needed the problems. They lived in an enormous gothic castle in the south of France called Dundrinkingginandslimlinetonicwithicebutnolemonin, which was originally built by Marco Polo for himself and a few friends he wanted to invite round to his place after the pub closed – an awe-inspiring construction of granite and bits of wood, with sweeping lawns recently modified to include an ornamental malaria swamp. He felt a sharp stab of steel in his groin and the sickening sensation of the warm ooze of blood welling up inside his flying jacket. A screaming hail of bullets punched through his left ear as he mused, 'Hey that was my ear'. Thinking this over, he continued to massage the coconut milk into her firm young breasts. He took another mouthful, letting it dribble slowly onto the tip of each erect nipple, and watched it stream tantalizingly down towards the moistly quivering lips of her French poodle, Kipper[1]. At the age of two years and nine months[2] I was in Ibiza, but much more of that anon[3].

The preceding page is obviously unreliable, so today's co-author[4] has suggested that we ought to clarify a few points:

DATE OF BIRTH: 8TH JAN 1941
SEX: MALE
CHRISTENED: GRAHAM
PLACE OF BIRTH: LEICESTER
STAR SIGN: CAPRICORN
FAVOURITE FOOD: CURRY
LEAST FAVOURITE FOOD: POISON
FAVOURITE POISON: GALLAMINE TRIETHIODIDE
FAVOURITE ANTIDOTE: NEOSTIGMINE

---

1. This particular passage could be totally untrue.
2. This is a lie. I was twenty-five.
3. See footnote 1 on previous page.
4. Oh, by the way, does that mean I can take tomorrow off? (A.)[5]
5. No. (G.)

EDUCATED AT: RAVENHURST ROAD. MIXED INFANT AND JUNIOR SCHOOL; SOUTH WIGSTON JUNIOR BOYS; KIBWORTH GRAMMAR SCHOOL; MELTON MOWBRAY GRAMMAR SCHOOL; EMMANUEL COLLEGE CAMBRIDGE; THE REGAL AND HISTORIC HOSPITAL OF ST SWITHINS (LONDON); YALE AND HARVARD; SANDHURST; A LITTLE KNOWN WELSH FINISHING SCHOOL. 8 'O' LEVELS .... NONE OF THEM IN GEOGRAPHY, WOODWORK OR ANYTHING WET LIKE THAT. CHEATED IN LATIN; 4 'A' LEVELS (ZOOL. BOT. PHYS. CHEM.) 2 'S' LEVELS (ZOOL & CHEM) B.A. 2.2. HONOURS DEGREE IN NATURAL SCIENCES. M.A. FOR WHICH I PAID £10; MB. B.Chir.

GENERAL MEDICAL COUNCIL REGISTRATION NO: 0136622
PASSPORT NO: 2
SHOE SIZE: 10
CHEST MEASUREMENT: 42"
HAT SIZE: 7 1/4
WAIST MEASUREMENT: 32"
INSIDE LEG MEASUREMENT: FAR TOO OBVIOUS A SET-UP FOR A CHEAP JOKE. CO-AUTHORS ARE NOT INDISPENSABLE.

I now think that my co-author may have been wrong in trying to clear up these details. All this is necessitated by the fact that, though I'm trying to write a history of my whole life, my home life in Leicester was so zzzzzzzzzzzzzzzzzzzzzzzzzzz. . . . oh, sorry, where was I? Oh yes, I mean all it was really was the usual humdrum wetting of nappies, later pants; not being allowed to sit next to Lottie the Czechoslovakian girl because I once shat myself; seeing bits of people hanging from trees – oh, that does sound interesting, perhaps I should put that down. I was three at the time and my mother wanted to take me along to see my father being a policeman, which is something he did most days. . . .

A street in Wigston Magna 1944. There has just been an

explosion in an aircraft in which nine Free Polish airmen had been flying. The force of the explosion has reduced them to their component parts and one can see quite clearly a lung hanging down from the lower branches of a chestnut tree, a leg on a front lawn, and a hole in the roof of a semi-d., which was later explained by a lady who came out of the house carrying a bucket with what looked like liver in it. The three-year-old boy is not particularly worried because he is holding his mummy's hand, and his daddy is in charge, and being very efficient about trying to sort out bits of human flesh into at least nine different sacks. Unfortunately there seem to be only eight heads and no other suspicious roof-holes.

Mummy calls out to Daddy, 'Walter . . .'

'Sorry dear, I'm busy. Hey you, that sack's already got two legs in it.'

Reflecting on this I go, 'Waaaaagggh' inwardly, and am just thinking of going, 'Waaaaagggh' outwardly when my mother grabs my hand.

'Walter dear, we were just out shopping and I thought that Graham might like . . .'

'Look dear, I'll see you later. Has anyone found that head yet? Hey! Has anyone in this street found a head? Come on, someone must have it, I know this street, you'd whip anything. . . . I mean, what the bloody hell are you going to do with a head?'

'Well dear, perhaps we'll go and get your tea.'

'What? Oh yes, egg on toast please. Left arm here, anyone missing a left arm?'

'We haven't got any eggs. There's a war on.'

'Ask Harold. Something's bound to have fallen off the back of a lorry.'

'All right, dear. Come on, Graham, stop staring at all that blood, it won't do you any good.'

'Oh come on, mum, this must be one of my major formative experiences. Waaaaaaaagggggghhhhhh. . . .!'

AND SO . . .

London, 1895. Oscar Wilde's residence. In the glittering drawing room are gathered a glittering group. The cream of London society . . . The Prince of Wales, James McNeill

A Street in Wigston Magna 1944

Whistler, George Bernard Shaw and Wilde himself are just a few of the notables present. Inevitably, it is Oscar Wilde that the party centres around. Raising his glass of champagne, the Prince speaks to his host.

'My congratulations, Wilde. Your play is a great success. The whole of London is talking about you.'

The group waits expectantly for the master of the paradox to be paradoxical. Wilde does not disappoint them.

'There is only one thing in the world worse than being talked about and that is not being talked about.'

For a full minute laughter reverberates around the room. Whistler turns puce with envy. Shaw twitches with jealousy. Aubrey Beardsley micturates in pique. Max Beerbohm stuffs a sour grape up his nostril and Jane Austen revolves in her grave.

The Prince claps Oscar on the shoulder. 'Very witty. Very, very witty.'

The game is afoot. Whistler takes a breath and ripostes:

'There is only one thing worse in the world than being witty and that is not being witty.'

It is a hit. The room rocks with laughter for another full minute. Oscar Wilde's face goes as green as his carnation. Shaw winces. Beardsley, feeling a pang of resentment, defecates in a riding boot. Beerbohm enviously punches a hole in a Chinese silk screen, and Jane Austen's false breast falls off. Wilde opines.

'I wish I had said that.'

Whistler smiles at him. He had expected that incisive retort and is ready for it.

'You will, Oscar. You will.'

Wilde waves an effete hand in the direction of Whistler.

'Your Highness, do you know James McNeill Whistler?'

Ducking the effete hand, the Prince declares, 'Yes, we play squash together.'

Wilde is in like a rapier.

'There is only one thing worse than playing squash together and that is playing it by yourself.'

He waits expectantly for the roars of laughter and the shrieks of glee. They do not come. The silence grows longer.

So does Shaw's beard. Eventually, Oscar mutters, 'I wish I hadn't said that.'

Seeing his bosom friend with egg on his face, Whistler cannot resist the temptation to throw an omelette.

'You did, Oscar. You did.'

The room rocks with laughter. Exhausted with the excellence of the wit and the gay bonhomie, the Prince bids his host farewell.

'You must forgive me Wilde, but I must get back up the Palace.'

Wilde is desperate. It's unheard of. The Prince of Wales leaving with a smile on his face that had not been put there by Oscar Wilde. He blurts:

'Your Majesty, you are like a big jam doughnut with cream on top.'

A shocked hush descends on the room. The Prince of Wales, like his mother on a previous occasion, is not amused.

'I beg your pardon.' Wilde splutters, completely at a loss. 'Er . . . er . . . er . . . er . . . it was one of Whistler's.'

The game is now not merely afoot. It's putting the boot in.

'I didn't say that.'

'You did, James, you did.'

The Prince of Wales and the assembled company gaze expectantly at Whistler. For a moment the celebrated painter is at a loss, and then . . .

'I meant that, like a doughnut, your arrival gives us pleasure, and your departure makes us hungry for more.'

Loud laughter and applause follow this elegant explanation. Encouraged, Whistler moves onto the attack.

'Your Majesty is like a stream of bat's piss.'

Over the gasps, the Prince of Wales thunders.

'I beg your pardon?'

Coolly the painter gazes at the Prince. 'It was one of Wilde's.'

How will the hero of a thousand cul-de-sacs cope with this one? The gathering does not have to wait long for an answer. The mind that has been sharpened to a sword's edge through years of verbal fencing rises brilliantly to the occasion.

'It sodding well wasn't. It was one of Shaw's.'

Bernard Shaw totters visibly as the buck that has been passed to him hangs heavily round his neck. But this is the man destined to write *Arms and the Man* and its astonishing sequel, *Armpits and the Woman*. Smiling at the Prince, he speaks softly.

'I merely meant, Your Majesty, that you shine out like a shaft of gold when all around is dark.'

There is a ripple of awed admiration. The ease with which Shaw has escaped from the sinking ship has been remarkable.

Shaw has been put on his mettle by a fellow Irishman and to Shaw a fellow Irishman is fair game. He gives Wilde a wicked look, then coolly drops the doyen of distinguished society in the ordure.

'Your Majesty is like a dose of clap.'

There is a collective gasp of horror. The horror becomes near panic, when Shaw, not waiting for the Prince's superb rejoinder of: 'I beg your pardon?' continues, 'Before you arrive is pleasure, but after a pain in the dong.'

The Prince of Wales pales in anger, and, as there is a lot of him, there's a lot of pale.

'What!!!' he shrieks.

Then Shaw plays his master card.

'It was one of Wilde's.'

Every eye in the room looks at Oscar Wilde, including the blood-shot pair belonging to the Prince of Wales.

'I'm waiting, Wilde. I'm waiting. . . .'

New York, 1976. The City Centre Theatre. A packed house. *Monty Python's Flying Circus* is appearing. We are in mid-sketch. Whistler is being played by John Cleese. Shaw is being played by Michael Palin. The Prince of Wales is being played by Terry Jones. I am playing Oscar Wilde. And I have just dried. I cannot remember the next line. The entire theatre waits. And, as they wait, so do I for that damned line to enter my head. It refuses to come but many other pieces of the past do. . . .

Hampstead, 1968. (Actually Belsize Park 1969, but Hampstead sounds better, and God knows why I bothered to lie about it being 1968, it's so pointless, isn't it?) Somewhere in

NW 3 in the latter half of the twentieth century, when everyone was being either homosexual, black, or a drug addict, and a compulsory part of the English course at Warwick University was sleeping with Germaine Greer – whose grading system ran from 'First Class, with Distinction' to 'You Weren't Going to Do It with THAT, were you?' – I first started to have trouble with embedded relative clauses. To describe this period I personally invented the word 'trendy'. (This is not the same word 'trendy' which had been in common parlance for yonks, but an entirely new word which actually means the same thing.) This new word 'trendy' was pronounced with extra emphasis on the 'N', though it was considered 'untrendy' (another of my linguistic inventions designed to replace the obsolete word 'untrendy', but carrying the same meaning) to make this slight shift of emphasis apparent and so no one actually pronounced it this way at all and only two close friends and John Lennon[1] were aware of the profound change I had perpetrated in the etymological fabric of the English Language. Many other words coined by myself were often to be heard in use at parties of the period, such as this one which took place in a large room somewhere in Belsize Park. . . .

A liquid light show is being projected onto the rear half of a giraffe which is protruding through the wall opposite the door. Everyone is shouting at everyone else in an attempt to make themselves heard over the ear-shattering noise of a fashionably unknown group.

'Excuse me,' I say, trying to push my way to the bar past a person trying to look casual whilst wearing a glittering codpiece and an albino cobra wound round his neck. His

1. It may seem that I am merely dropping names here and in fact I am. I've never met John Lennon in my life. But who needs him when you have been raised in the same street as people like Nilsson, H.; Starr, R.; Harrison, G.; John, E.; Floyd, Pink; Zeppelin, Led; Moon, K.; Johns, Capt. WE (Retd.); Bowie, D.; Clarke, Pet; Arabia, Lawrence of; Shankar, Ravi; Menuhin, Yehudi; West, Mae; Distel, S.; Ali, M.; Mother, H.R.H. The Queen; Durrells, L. and G.; Fields, Gracie; Coward, N., and seventeen Nobel prizewinners? But see D. Niven's, *The Moon is a Baboon*, where he tries to avoid the charge of name-dropping by a rather clumsy pretence at humility: 'I just happened to know them. . . .' Cut it out, Dave. When it's time for grovelling leave it to the expert.

fluorescent face seems to be painted like a Coca Cola tin, and it's impossible not to notice that he is wearing a pale green palette rinse.

'That's nice,' I say.

'Thanks,' he trendily replies.

'Is the bar over there?'

'Oh how orgasmic darlingarama-ette, what a divinely hairy chest.'

'Thanks. Nice to talk to you.'

'I wonder when Roy Orbison will die?'

'Quite.'

At this point a man wearing a suit made entirely of wood is wheeled over my toe, and I look around to find David and see that he's stuck talking to a group of people dressed entirely in leather, except for their spectacles which are made of glass and leather. He seems happily occupied so I continue to hunt for a drink. Someone shouts—

'For Christ's sake, Beryl, stop necking with that dog.'

'But it's an Alsatian . . .'

'So?'

I suddenly spot a gin bottle, but the space between me and it is largely occupied by a forty-stone negress wearing a linnet feather, who screams,

'This place ain't cool enough[1] for me, man, I'm going.'

At this point she shoots herself through the left temple with a rather nice Alan Aldridge-designed derringer. There is a chorus of, 'Bye darling!'

'But she shot herself,' a novice screams.

'Hype down Clovissa.'

The gin bottle is now streaming with fresh warm blood and there is a piece of frontal lobe lodged in the only available glass. I remember my medical training and leave.

Very few seconds later, David and I are outside. It's a warm

---

1. 'Enough': Zambian pronunciation, popular in Hampstead at this time, of the name Enoch, here referring to Enoch Blomqvist. The word 'Blomqvist' was currently very much in vogue amongst Icelandic apiarists and carried the meaning 'sufficiency in quantity of'. It was commonly used in phrases such as 'Just one of you little buggers sting me again and I'll napalm the lot of you. I've had quite blomqvist of it, do you hear?'

summer evening, the moon is beaming, the streets are empty, the odours of rose bay willow herb, night-scented stock and dogshit vie with each other to find soft purchase on our nasal membranes, here in Belsize Avenue. Everything is calm and peaceful.

We are happily walking down the street when our path is partly obstructed by a large peony bush that hangs over it from behind someone's garden fence. I push the low hanging bush away with just a hint of irritation.

'Don't be so rough, they're pretty . . .'

'What are?'

'The peonies,' says David, picking one. 'Look . . .'

Instantly a police siren wails and there is a screech of brakes with dust flying everywhere as a police-car slams to a halt beside us and two policemen leap out. One of them, the brains of the outfit, grabs the peony from David and says,

'What's this then?'

'A peony,' I say.

'Oh you admit that then?'

The second policeman is already beginning to write in his notebook.

'Admit? But look, officer . . .'

'Don't try to flatter me, you won't get out of it that way.'

'Get out of what?' (Exasperation creeping in.)

'Calm down,' says the larger policeman with the notebook.

'Look, please, what am I supposed to have done?'

'Not you, him,' pointing at David. 'He's committed a felony.'

I am beginning to get irritated. 'What do you mean?'

'Theft. That's what I mean. He has taken away the personal goods of another, viz. one peony . . .'

'But it's only a flower.'

'Only a flower!' hyperboles the notebooked policeman. 'Ho! Ho!'

'That is Property,' points out his companion (with enough emphasis not to have needed the additional heavy 'Property' from his colleague).

'What do you mean, "Property"?' I said.

'Did that peony just appear out of thin air?'

'What's this then?'

'No, it came from that bush.'

'That bush eh? Is that bush his?' Pointing at David.

'No.'

'Is it yours?'

'No.'

'Is it the bush of a friend or relation of yours?'

'No.'

'Then it is Another's. Did you ask the permission of Another?' he added, indicating the house to which the bush belonged.

'No.'

'That, my lad, is theft, which is a felony and punishable with up to thirty years imprisonment. . . .'

In my mind's eye, further up the street I see an old lady being beaten up by four thugs and innocent passers-by being attacked and robbed. Several blatant rapes occur, while men wearing black and white hooped sweaters and masks run in and out of houses carrying huge bags marked 'loot'.

'What do you mean? Theft! Felony! He just picked a flower,' I say angrily.

'Stole a flower!'

'All right, then we'll give it back.'

'You can't, lad. It's severed.'

'What do you mean, "severed"?'

'Well, did you intend to put it back?'

'Er, yes, all right, we did.'

'Ho! And how would you do that, sir?'

'Well I think I'd, er . . .'

'Sellotape? Nail it back? A few well-placed rivets? You couldn't, could you?'

'Well no, I s'pose not.'

'Well there you are. 'Course if you'd taken the whole bush, pulled it up roots and all, we couldn't have proved that you didn't intend to put it back.'

A few streets away a President is being assassinated.

'All right, look, this is ridiculous. I'll buy a whole new bush for them.'

'Well it wouldn't be the same bush, would it?'

33

The second policeman stops taking notes, in order to 'loom' larger and be in for the kill.

'Look, I'll just go and ask the owner of the house whether he minds our having taken a peony and if he does mind I'll pay him compensation, but of course he won't mind – anyway the thing was obstructing the pavement. . . .'

'Don't try to be clever with us my lad . . .'

The policeman who has the notebook raises one fist. His colleague pushes it down saying, 'Not yet, not yet,' under his breath. Finally I lose patience.

'Haven't you anything better to do? There are murders going on, arson, rapes and here's *two* of you just worried over one bloody peony . . .'

'Oh, so we've got a difficult one here, have we? Sergeant?'

He calls over to the car, out of which leaps a sergeant who strides over.

'Look mate, do you want to come up the station and be "interviewed"?'

'Can be very nasty, being "interviewed" . . .' adds the man with the notebook.

'Are you threatening violence?' I ask, raising my umbrella slightly to emphasize my point.

'Right, right,' says the sergeant. 'Send for reinforcements.'

At this point the first policeman takes out his radio intercom. 'There's been a peony-severance in Belsize Lane, can we have reinforcements . . .?'

We walk briskly off leaving them to it. They are far too involved with the due processes of the law to notice. All over London police cars are radioing in to H.Q. with messages like: 'Am proceeding in an easterly direction along North End Avenue towards the scene of a peony-severance on the South side of Belsize Lane. . . .' Sirens screech, men leap out of Black Marias, water cannons are brought out. Questions are asked in Parliament, and then in the Hague. Finally the whole matter cannot be resolved without the kindly intervention of my old friend, Dr Kurt Waldheim from the Jolly Old U.N. Building Here in New York. Pretty neat, don't you think? . . .

A few doors and a brief time-warp away at the City Centre,

New York 1976, an expectant crowd still waits for the Wildean riposte . . . I am beginning to break out into a sweat. The line just won't come. John Cleese shuffles uncomfortably and mutters, 'Get on with it.'

Thinking this is a prompt I proclaim loudly: 'Get on with it!'

The reaction of the audience gives me the definite impression that this is not my line. It's at moments like this, when one thinks, 'Oh fuck it! Does it all really matter? What are we all here for? Are we predestined to take the paths we follow?' And sure enough, as though to prove a point, I was actually in Los Angeles a year later. . . .

We extinguished our cigarettes and fastened our seat belts, then did it again in French and Spanish, as the first class lounge of the mighty British Airways Boeing 747 banked sharply to the left. Captain Chet Bigglesburg's crisp Oxford drawl slid powerfully through the intercom: 'Listen, yawl. What ho, how are you all, yawl? Anyway, jolly good! We'll be . . . um, like . . . sort of landing and things in sort of, yawl, Los Angeles in approximately sort of fifteen minutes from this point-style moment in time, instance-wise, yawl. That is to say landingization will be completed sort of . . . in a bit . . . as of now, yawl. . . . Toodle-pip . . . sort of . . . what . . . oh!' Click. 'Frightfully sorry – yawl.' Click.

The enormous bar glid to a halt and I and my financial adviser, Major Sloane, were ushered from our divans by the by now nude Cypriot debutante air hostess. She offered us our disembarkation executive foot modules, vinylized nylonette uppers, hand-stitched onto personalized red-carpetlette soles – a touching modern reminder of a never-existent old-world charm.

In our sixty-foot four-seater Cadillac we executived off downtown for the première of Mohammed Ali's film *The Greatest*, an excellent movie – a damn sight better than *Jaws* or *Saturday Night Fever* – which was rejected by black and white audiences alike for simply telling the truth. Or could the distributors have found its portrayal of parasitical white middlemen uncomfortably astute?

The select open-air reception afterwards in the vast Plaza

de los Reaganos drew a huge crowd of spectators, all eager to see the champ arrive stylishly by helicopter. All eyes gazed heavenwards as Mohammed Ali in a typical flamboyant gesture, walked quietly in from the back and mingled with the guests. He was soon spotted by hordes of film, television and press cameramen who would have made personal contact impossible, had he not politely ignored them. Like any decent actor, he simply wanted to know how the film had gone.

As at all film premières, most people were standing around trying to look as if they knew the star so well that they didn't even need to acknowledge his presence, and merely peered around wondering whether anyone had noticed *them*. Five people were so famous they didn't even need to turn up, and their vacant spaces were stared at with awe. *There* was going to be Sammy Davis Jr., and over *there* would have been Frank Sinatra, if his trichologist hadn't ordered him to sit at home in a chair. The other boxing aficionados were so indescribably famous they had had to hire three separate stadiums to be absent at.

I had never seen so much awe. I left them all to it, and congratulated the man himself on a great performance. He knew that I meant what I had said, and we sat down and chatted for twenty minutes. I found him kind, perceptive and wise and, unlike some who pass for intelligent, capable of listening to others. He must have seen something in me too, otherwise I wouldn't have lasted the full twenty minutes. We talked about religion, black and gay liberation, and the fear that drives man to destroy man – certainly one of the most fascinating conversations in my life. But the gin that had given me the courage to talk to him in the first place also made me completely forget everything that we said. What a wasted opportunity! Sorry everybody, but Major Sloane is trying to arrange a return bout on more equal terms, now that I'm back in training.

I thanked The Greatest, we shook hands, and I walked back into the crowd. My head was buzzing. Everything went beige with little patches of russet. I was aware of a sensation of violent speed as I was crushed by gigantic G forces against the granite steps of the David Niven memorial which seemed to be hurtling out into the black abyss of space.

'This is no time for musing,' I mused. Suddenly it seemed that a hole had been torn in the very fabric of space. Was I being sucked into a black hole rent in the great doughnut of eternity? 'Don't be silly,' I thought. 'Of course you are.' It was almost as if I was being drawn along a powerful tractor beam towards some unearthly giant star ship. As luck would have it I was.

'Well, well, well, this is a turn up,' I said to myself, thinking, 'What a strange thing to say.' It must have been my upbringing which brought about my following action, for at moments of great stress I always think of bits of people hanging in trees. I threw up. Small bits of tomato skin, sweet corn husks and diced carrot moved out into an elliptical orbit about the sun. There before me was an immense cylindrical structure, oblate in cross section, 9·2 km. long, 1·92 km. across its longer elliptical axis and 1·56 km. down its shorter elliptical axis. Its further end seemed to be glowing with eerie incandescent power, and the brown, fluted, longitudinal striations made it look for all the world like a lighted Peter Stuyvesant that had just been gently sat on by someone wearing slightly damp corduroy trousers, but twice as sinister. The force beam in which I was trapped was still drawing me and the miniscule portion of what had once been Los Angeles into an entrance bay in what would have been the middle section of the filter tip if it had actually been a cigarette as described and not a bloody great space ship.

As usual in these situations, I now lost consciousness, being overcome with horror at the thought of all the descriptive detail that would otherwise have been needed. Everything went black – absolutely everything. I couldn't see a damn thing but utter blackness until I suddenly woke up out of my extremely well thought-out insensibility, and found myself on the bridge of the star ship, which, as luck would have it, was completely indescribable. I slowly became aware of a strange group of totally unimaginable (my luck was still holding) creatures crowded round a cluster of scanning screens. To my astonishment I saw that they were watching fictional re-runs from my encounter with puberty (what we doctors refer to as Chapter Two).[1]

1. This is a rather personal footnote from Graham Chapman addressed *in strictest confidence* to Alex G. Martin and David J. Sherlock. . . . It's difficult to pin down, but while there have been some quite interesting passages in this chapter, it all seems a bit *disjointed* and self-conscious (the footnotes especially). Normally I would be the last person to discourage anything 'zany', 'off-the-wall', 'mason-joshing' – call it what you will[2] – but in this case I am perturbed. It could be that we are taking the goodwill of the reader too much for granted. This *is* supposed to be an autobiography. Given that, how do we explain:
  (i) No attempt to present a logical time sequence?
 (ii) A whole section shamelessly lifted from a television sketch which was never performed on stage anyway?
(iii) Profitless and unwelcome forays into the realms of science fiction? 'Any fool can gaze at the stars – it takes wit to live in the gutter.' (Emil Zatopek).
(iv) Five authors?
It seems to me that Point (iv) is the cruncher. The time has come to streamline our authorship personnel and allow some of us to leave. To be scrupulously fair I placed all five names in a hat and, blindfold, made a random selection. With some regret, I have to inform you that Douglas Adams, Charles Thing, David A. Yallop and Michael Object, will no longer be with us. But calamity is, as they say, the great-aunt of feeling a bit better after a while, and I hope that you are looking forward as much as I am to a straightforward well written, factual *Chapter Two*.[4]
  2. Hate 'off-the-wall.' (D.)[3]
  3. I like 'Mason-joshing'. (A.)
  4. Yup. (D. and A.)

CHAPTER TWO

Eton

Summer Term (or 'Wops' as we called it) seemed to have dragged on endlessly. I sat there in a faded deck-chair, gazing dreamily at the shimmering greensward which I had come to know so well. 'Clop,' came the sound of Clement Attlee Jr. hitting another four. Though only a Prime Minister's son, he'd managed to fit in quite well with some of the other boys, and was regarded as 'simply ozzard' by the Sen. Co. Prae. I suppose that was because he never got 'wazzed',[1] although he had gronked most of the lower school with his tadger.

'Clop' – yet another four. I thought of Horace – *Iam victoria, tam facilis, scrotum non valet.* We always beat Harrow anyway – why bother? I stood up with languid ease.

A junior tick came up, and, tugging at my flannels, grovelled, 'Oh, Chapman, sir, may I clean your teeth tonight, oh please?'

'Why don't you bugger off, shagspot?' I replied tradi-

1. Old Salopian for being afraid. (See Robert Graves, *The Greek Myths*).

tionally, and gave him a sharp clip on the temple with my bat.

'Thank you sir,' he sobbed, and traditionally slumped to the ground.

'Plucky little squit, that young Macmillan, should go far,' I thought.

The sun dappled through the copper-tinted leaves of the beeches along 'Big Wall' as I walked back. 'Lower Downers' seemed strangely calm in that light. Far from the sweltering pitch, it stood like an oasis of quietude in its granite thisness. The air was still, save for the drone of a distant one-seater. Where was it travelling from? Where to? Did it matter? The smell of freshly-mown grass wafted over from far off Hayes Meadow, the village clock chimed in the distance, and somewhere, miles above our petty earth, a wisp of cloud took flame from the dying embers of the setting sun. They combined to produce an atmosphere so redolent of this type of writing.

A faint 'clop' in the distance splintered the fabric of my meditations. A crass intrusion. 'What the hell,' I thought. 'Just for that I shall bloody well bogle up Mikla Passage, and if I meet the Captain of Montem "collecting" "salt" or some "lobsters" "bartering" in the "foricas", I shan't give an Oppidan's "fart".'

I cycled past rows of parental Rolls-Royces, cheap-looking Bentleys, lower-middle Daimlers, and Cadillacs NQOC.[1] In a few days I would be in Nice, soaking up the sun at the side of my father's pool, while Jenkins hovered by with a tray of vodkatinis. Someone shouted, 'Hey! Look where you're going!' I looked round to see who it was, and 'Clop!!!' . . . Everything went beige, with purple bits round the edges. The acrid smell of burning rubber, a stabbing pain in my shoulder, mists swirling before my eyes, and the distant sound of waves crashing on the shore, suddenly stopped.

'Would you like another sandwich, dear?'
'What?'
'They're your favourite, sandwich spread.'
'So this is Nice . . .'

1. Not Quite Our Class.

I look round. Can it be Nice? We are sitting in our Ford Anglia, my father, my mother and myself, on the Promenade, and all we can see is rain, grey sky, grey sea, and grey waves crashing over a grey sea wall.

'What d'you mean Nice? This is Scarborough. You do too much reading,' says my father. My mother agrees: 'It'd do you more good if you ate your tea.'

'Quite right. You can't get through to him when he's got a book in his hand. What is it anyway?'

'I haven't been reading.'

'What's that then?'

My father leans over and glances at a few lines of the paperback that lies open in my hands. Unfortunately he chooses a paragraph in which two centurions are caressing each other in bed. (That sort of thing quite obviously did not go down well with the police force in those days.) I wobble a little and close the book.

'It's a history book.'

'That's a bee funny sort of a history book. Put it away.'

'What is it dear?' my mother asks.

'Nothing, dear. Put it away, Graham. Don't let your mother see that.'

'What is it?' she insists. I turn to her and explain, 'It's called *Claudius the God* by Robert Graves – a fine historical reconstruction of the life of Claudius, the republican Roman Emperor, thought of in his time as a pitiful fool, though the reign Mr Graves describes is far from folly.'

'Is it? Harumph!' says my father, as he locks the book in the glove-compartment.

'Graves . . . Graves . . . wasn't he born in Wimbledon?' asks my mother.

'No that was Tim Graves.'

'No it wasn't, you remember the Graves. There was Alf, and he married that Amalia von Ranke, a bonny woman. They used to live . . . er, above the chemist in Thurbid Street, opposite the Gantlets.'

'I never did like the Gantlets – that smelly corgi of theirs. Should have had it put down.'

'They should. Pitiful. Its back legs didn't work. Anyway,

'*It's called* Claudius the God'

finish your tea. We ought to go and get that haddock for Mrs Riches.'

'There's plenty of time for that later on. Thraxted's doesn't close till five.'

'They're bound to be out of haddock by then.'

'Well, get halibut.'

'Mrs Riches asked specially for haddock.'

'Haddock, halibut, cod – there's no difference. It's all fish. Let's just sit here for a bit and enjoy the view.

'It's raining,' I say.

'It's bracing. You should have your window open, lad. Get a bit of ozone into your lungs.'

'Ozone is oxygen in a condensed state, having three atoms to the molecule. O_3. What you can smell is rotting seaweed.'

'Well, it's good for you.'

'No it isn't.'

'Don't argue with your father.'

'It's these fancy books he's been reading. You can't learn everything out of books my lad.'

'There is no argument. It's a fact.'

'Stop it, Graham. Come on we'll go and get the fish.'

'No we won't. We'll stay here. Open that window and get some fresh air into your lungs.'

My father lights his pipe. The familiar scent of burning rubber fills the car. I cough and open the window, getting a faceful of wind and rain, followed quickly by two and a half pints of icy North Sea.

'I think we should go and get the fish.'

'That ship out there,' says my father, 'is bringing wood from Norway. Coniferous wood, used in the paper-manufacturing industry since the late fifteenth century. The process was originally invented in China by Ts'ai Lun around about A.D. 105, but the first paper mill in England was owned by John Tate in Hertford. The manufacture of continuous lengths, however . . .'

'Oh the Tates! Wasn't their youngest walking about with that Valerie Maskell?'

'No.'

'Yes he was, the one that took ballet lessons for her fallen arches.'

'No. This process was developed by the stationers, Messrs H. and S. Fourdrinier. . . .'

'It *was* her. You remember, she was the one that got all the spots at secretarial college.'

'Quiet, Edith. The Fourdriniers were assisted in this by Mr Brian Donkin, an inventor and engineer.'

'Donkin! Wasn't his step-uncle Stephanie a wholesale poulterer in Peatling Parva?'

'No.'

'Yes he was – it was their youngest that moved downstairs next door to the chemists in Wimbledon, nearly opposite the Gantlets.'

'Shut up! D'you realize that if you look out there on a very clear day you can't quite see Denmark? And if you look over there, you would almost catch a glimpse of France if it weren't invisible. Oh, the sea!'

'I think we should get the haddock.'

'Will you shut up about that bloody haddock!'

'Why is it that every bloody year . . .'

'Language!'

'. . . . Every year, our summer holiday consists of two weeks in Scarborough, Filey or Bridlington, sitting in a car in the rain, bickering. Why don't we go to bloody Denmark . . . ?'

'Language! It's the toilets.'

'What?! What toilets?'

'Your father can't bear foreign toilets.'

'But he's never been abroad!'

'Your Uncle Harry was in North Africa during the war and their toilets – ugh!'

'But we're talking about DENMARK! Their sanitary facilities make ours look primitive.'

'I suppose you read that in *Hygiene in Denmark* by Rupert bloody Graves.'

'We did promise haddock.'

'Oh all right! We'll go and get your bloody flaming bloody bloody haddock. The trouble with you two is that you don't appreciate the beauties of nature.'

We drive off through a moderate to heavy spume.

'What's that you've got over there?' my father barks.

'It's a book,' I counter.

'What book?' comes his brusque reply.

'*I, Biggles*, by Captain W. E. Graves,' I riposte.

'Captain, eh? That sounds better,' he re-ripostes, and slams the engine into third. . . .

The plane banked sharply to the left as we hurtled downwards, but the Fokker Wolf was still on our tail.

'A-a-a-a-a-a-a-zing,' went the twin cowl-mounted Mittelschmertz 25 mm cannons.

'Peng!' it went, in German, as one of the shells bit into the sleek wooden fuselage.

'Peng?' cogitated Biggles. 'That's the German for "Bang!"'

'We've been hit,' volunteered Ginger grimly.

'Nothing,' said Biggles grimlier, as he slipped his leather-gloved hand over the by now moistened joystick. He pulled it back in a series of sharp jerks.

'Level off a mo,' put in Algy drily and through drawn lips; stepped purposefully into the body of the aircraft, past the by now shapely nude lady navigator; and back into the rear of the plane. The door of the Gents Only Sauna hung precariously from one hinge. He slammed it shut with a haunting squawk, and fought his way past the two naked WAFs wrestling in perfumed sump-oil. He erupted into the Aft Leather Room, to find Wingco still chained to a cross, wearing the by now familiar black hood bearing the also familiar Wing Commanderic braid.

'Have your way with me, you hunk of manhood,' he hinted coyly.

'What ho, old sport!' hazarded Algy gingerly. 'I say, old man, the Group's a bit dashed worried – thinks you might have some kind of, well . . . you know, problem . . . you old bison. . . .' He fingered his cigarette nervously.

'Don't worry about me, old tapir, I've pulled through a lot worse than this.'

The plane lurched suddenly as Biggles swerved to avoid a hail of bullets that pumped in spurts out of the penis-like nosecone of the pursuing Fokker. Algy rushed for'ard.

'Everything OK, Skipper?' he admitted.

'We haven't made it yet,' inserted Biggles, as he gritted his thighs and plunged his machine into a savage spin.

As they plunged downwards, the mighty engines throbbed and the well-lubricated pistons thrust themselves back and forth in their vice-like steel sheaths.

'You look a bit green around the gills, old eland,' observed Biggles smoothly.

'Never felt better,' puked Algy. 'Sorry about the mess,' he opined.

'Why can't you just *say* things?' snorted Biggles. 'Tell you what, old man, having a bit of trouble with this one, could you just pop your hand down my Mae West?'

'If it's an order, old guillemot.'

'It is,' grinned Biggles.

'Right-ho, here it comes.' Algy plunged a questing sensitive hand into the Group Captain's flying jacket.

The plane soared upwards.

'Don't stop now, I'm nearly there.'

'So am I.'

'Oooooh!'

'Aaaaah!'

'Ooo-ooh!' ejaculated Biggles and Algy together. They were through. The white silence of a cloud surrounded them.

'What about me?' rasped Ginger.

'Fuck off a sec. Ooooh,' oohed Biggles and Algy. Then suddenly they were through it. Peace. Calm. Ecstasy. They floated, as one, in a post-what can't be described in a children's book sort of feeling.

Ginger had missed out again, but he was used to this, and easing himself back into his cold leather chair, mused, 'To heck with the lot of 'em, I'll just jolly well sit down here and improve the bally old mind a little, don't you know?'

Languidly he cold-chiselled his way through the padlock on his Air Survival Reading Kit and snapped the seal of the 2·5 ml. phial containing Tincture of Cricket Pavilion. He clicked it neatly into the 'glue-sniffing' socket on his oxygen mask and ran his rapidly glazing eyes over the Emergency Inflight Reading list. *The Complete Works of Captain W. E. Johns, How to Speak English in Other Languages, The Interpretation of Dreams* by Sigmund Freud. . . .

'It is,' grinned Biggles

'That's dashed odd,' he thought. 'Hun Yid Lit.! Must have a gander. . . .' Cautiously he opened the volume, and gasped as he read inside the cover, 'Happy Barmitzvah, Algernon, old ocelot, keep off the pork, love Aunt Rachel already, what?' So that's why Algy always wore his swimming-togs in the showers! The flipping bounder!

As the subtle aroma of grass-clippings, blancoed canvas, and linseed oil swathed his olfactory organs, he flicked through the pages with curiosity. . . . ' "Theories of Dreaming and Its Function". Mmm,' flick-flick, he went. . . . ' "Symbols in Dreams". Mmm . . . no. . . . "Sexual Symbols in Dreams". Mmm. . . . no. . . . "Sexual Symbols in Breams"? Mmm . . . maybe. . . .' . . . Then 'thwack!' It was as if he had been struck nose before wicket by a cricket-box hurled at full stench. . . . ' "NAVIGATIONAL DREAMS" – Spot on, chocks away!' he enthused, and read hungrily on:

'In the following pages I shall prove that the entire psychology of man can only be understood with reference to the science of navigation. ["Quite right," interposed Ginger.] I remember a thirty-five-year-old patient whose pre-pubertal son was having recurrent nightmares in which he would push a raspberry up his left nostril and run into the middle of the lounge shouting "Pelmets!" This caused such embarrassment that his father punished him by making him stand on a window-ledge holding a whole punnet of raspberries. They became so heavy that he lost his balance and fell down the face of a huge white cliff in the shape of a gendarme's nose, after which he woke up to find himself inexplicably in the sea at the bottom of a cliff. In later discussions with the boy, it became apparent that to him the raspberries represented raspberries, and the cliff was in fact a cliff. But to the psycho-analyst, the cliff is a glaring symbol of a navigation-fetish.

'Man's life is divided into two phases: 1 Childhood, and 2 Navigation. Childhood is divided into the following stages: (i) Heavy petting navigation; (ii) Coital navigation; (iii) Embryonic navigation; (iv) Foetal navigation; (v) Neo-natal navigation; (vi) Infantile navigation; (vii) the Pre-pubertal navigational spurt; (viii) Pubertal navigational day; and (ix)

Post-pubertal navigation – beginning of marine period (onset of *Regenwettertraum*[1]).

At this point we come into the longer phase, Navigation (2), which we may divide, with *Aesculapius, Galen, Patanjali, Nietzsche, Marx, Len Deighton,* and *Hitler's dog,* into:

 2 (i) At sea
 2 (ii) On land
 2 (iii) In the air
 2 (iv) Other places

' "2 (i) Navigation at sea" may be divided into the following broad categories:

 2 (i) (α) On top of the sea
 2 (i) (β) Under it
 2 (i) (γ) Quite close to the sea, but not actually getting your feet wet (*Schwuhlwasserfussbeklei-dungnichtgestellt*)[2]

' "2 (i) (α) Navigation on top of the sea" can be further divided into:

 2 (i) (α) (Ж) On top of the sea in the Northern Hemisphere;
 2 (i) (α) (И) On top of the sea in the Southern Hemisphere;

For clarity I shall divide these into a further Four Categories:

1. There would appear to be no equivalent in our language for this Viennese peasant word. The nearest would, I suppose, be 'soggy dreams'.

2. This Viennese student pork-butcher's slang word means literally, 'My God, there goes a clever psychoanalyst'; it is also an allusion to *Twelve Bream in My Wellingtons* by Horatio Nelson (Adm.), a puzzling title which Freud was later brilliantly to interpret as 'an obvious apostolic complex' in which Nelson himself plays the Christ-figure: bream representing the early Christian fish-symbol, and at the same time an overt corruption of the word 'dream' quite common in navigational dreams ('bream', *vide supra*). 'He was also clearly in love with an as yet unborn military rubber fetishist.' Freud intended later to expand this footnote into twelve volumes, provisionally entitled, *Generals, Admirals, Oedipus, Vagina-Envy, Fish, Christ, Masturbation, Oh and all sorts of other things like Cucumbers, Radishes, Figs, Donkeys, Other People's Bottoms, Gall-Bladder Fixations, Teeth, Snow, Hash, Uppers, Downers, Bakelite Underwear, Sports Commentators, Pole-Vaulting, and the Great Vaseline Boom*; but sadly this was not to be. He died, leaving Tim Rice and Andrew Lloyd-Webber to translate it into the Broadway smash-hit, *Kiss My Twat*, an all-goat musical comedy.

2 (i) (α) (水) (矢) On top of the sea in the Western part of the Northern Hemisphere;

2 (i) (α) (水) (石) On top of the sea in the Eastern part of the Northern Hemisphere;

2 (i) α) (水) (獅) On top of the sea in the Western part of the Southern Hemisphere;

2 (i) (α) (水) (食) On top of the sea in the Eastern part of the Southern Hemisphere;

'The reader must be aware that this is only a crude classifi-
cation, good enough in the time of Magellan, but, since the
researches of Troublemächer, now revealed to be only the tip
of the penguin. The latter postulates the following:

2 (i) (a) (水) (矢) (🦅) On top of the sea in the
Northern part of the Western part of the Northern Hemisphere;

2 (i) (a) (水) (矢) (🐦) On top of the sea in the
Southern part of the Western part of the Northern
Hemisphere;

2 (i) (a) (水) (矢) (🐊) On top of the sea in the
Northern part of the Eastern part of the Northern
Hemisphere;

2 (i) (a) (水) (矢) (〗) On top of the sea in the
Southern part of the Eastern part of the Northern
Hemisphere;
And so on up to:

(2) (i) (α) (水) (矢) (开) On top of the sea in the
Southern part of the Eastern part of the Southern
Hemisphere.

'Since Troublemächer, however, tremendous strides have
been made in the field of geo-physics, in particular recogni-
tion of the shifting of the earth's magnetic poles, and it is
now considered more scientifically valid to be more geogra-
pho-specific. This leads us to a huge list, which is obviously
beyond the scope of this book to quote in full, but includes
the following:

230 Part of the Timor Sea known as Yampi Sound, off the North Part of Western Australia;

750,829 A portion of the sea 4½ km to the East of Platiyalos on the island of Mykonos (Gr.) known locally as: δ γιαλός ὅπου γυχνάζουν ὅλοι οἱ ξένοι τοιούτοι και ἑκοέτουν τὰ γεννητικὰ τους οργανα[1]

10³⁹⁵ A patch of sea 2 inches square, 59 metres along a line drawn between the institute of physics in Copenhagen and Bentley's ice-cream stall on the beach at Scarborough (Eng.)

10³⁹⁵ + 1 Beneath Biggles.'

'Beneath Biggles! That's damn clever,' he haemoptysized, and read on.

'In relation to this I remember a twenty-nine-year-old female patient whose exactly adolescent son was having recurrent dreams about flying. In one dream – which he was able to recall particularly vividly because he was on a youth-hostelling holiday in the Lake District, and his red-haired companion in the bunk above him had fallen asleep, dropping a navigational handbook, which spiralled down and struck him on the temple, causing the rapid onset of wakefulness – a fictional aviator called Bigglesworth and his companions are attempting to escape from a Fokker Wolf which is pursuing them and shooting at them. They are hit somewhere in the back of the plane and Algy (one of Biggles' companions) goes to inspect the damage. It is not serious. After a routine exchange with a Wing Commander in the rear compartment of the plane, he returns to the pilot's cabin to report that all is well. There his Group Captain is having trouble with his flying jacket, but with Algy's help manages to sort it out and escape the pursuing Fokker at the same time. A typical dream-recall of a particularly exciting episode in an adventure story for boys. Or so it would seem.

'Let us look at the dream more closely. The first thing we notice is that the description is full of overt references to changes in direction ("the plane *banked sharply to the left*",

1. Untranslatable, but means 'the beach where lots of foreign perverts go and wave their genitals about.'

2. This means 10 to the power of 395, and is not a footnote.

"the plane *lurched suddenly*", "Biggles *swerved* to avoid the pursuing Fokker"), an unmistakable symptom of navigational obsessions. Note also the use of zoological terminology in their navigational exchanges with one another ("old *bison*", "old *tapir*" and even "old *guillemot*"), clearly indicating a yearning for a pre-rational, animal state of existence, in which navigation was not yet distinguishable from simply running around. The boy patient clearly identifies himself with the minor character, Ginger, who is excluded from the adventure because he is navigationally inadequate.'

At this point Ginger stopped reading. 'Ginger?' he thought. 'That's me! Inadequate?' What a bally awful tome don't you know. What ho, old chap!' He slid back the bakelite window, and grinned through steel lips as he watched the book hurtle in a plinth-defying spiral towards an angry North Sea. . . .

'Clop!'

I had been struck on the head, causing rapid wakefulness. The Anglia was now parked outside Thraxted's fish shop, with my mother inside, engaged in the purchase of haddock, and my father saying,

'You've been bloody reading again!'

'I haven't.'

'Well what's this in my hand?'

'Oh, it's *The Interpretation of Dreams* by Sigmund Freud, probably his most original work, in which he discovered a way of exploring the unconscious and found that neurotic symptoms are like dreams in that they are a product of the conflict and compromise between the conscious and unconscious states. He was able to . . .'

'Is it?' he said, as he thumbed through the pages. 'What's this? . . . "As a little girl she remembered her older brother and his friends asking her to remove her undergarments and perform cartwheels, thus displaying her genitalia to their curious gaze. In later life she . . ." '

'I've got the haddock. What were you saying? What's that book?'

'Nothing.' The glove compartment opened and closed. 'Nothing, just a road-map.'

'Who's Freud then?'

'He's an expert on . . . navigation. He's very interesting, his theories of navigation, you see, longitude and latitude . . .'

'Ah well, that's enough of that. Let's get back to Mrs Riches with this haddock.'

'Right!'

Quite a lot happened over the next few years, a disastrous sexual experiment with Rita Blake; my first love affair with another boy; stuffing snails into a gatepost with Annette Hoy; the hen-stealing nuns; Pigshit Freeman; Miss Chamberlain's three consecutive head-girls pregnant; my questions about ejaculation to a biology master; Anthony Blond and a book called *Health and Hygiene for Secondary Schoolgirls*, written by myself and my brother; Albert the groundsman; me holding hands with Mark Collins in a maths class; the couple copulating in the French library; Painting John Willder black; 'Who knows Eskimo Nell?'; M'sieur le bog va pooh; purple smoke; little boys' eardrums; 'This is a raid'; and elderly spinsters wanking off birthday cakes – but such trivia need no elaboration. One childhood is much like another. Amateur psychologists who think it's clever to explain the character of the later man from a jumble of largely fictitious memories can ferret for their filth in other people's autobiographies. They have opened the wrong book.

CHAPTER THREE

Cambridge

Cambridge. A university town built in a featureless, flat landscape – so featureless and flat you wonder why anyone chose it as a location for anything. 'The magnificence of St John's, the noteworthy splendour of Trinity, the sheer pauntliness of "The Backs" . . . and, gazing at the magnificent, noteworthy, sheer splendour of the pauntly King's College Chapel, it would be a world-weary traveller indeed who did not pause to think, "Why the fuck didn't they build the whole town two inches to the right?" '

A fair, if somewhat rudely couched question, to which an answer may be found only by turning back the clocks of time. . . .

Let us imagine it is the year 1282. An urgent message arrives at the court of King Edward I. 'Most noble sire, I have built a bridge over the River Cam.' The royal reply, despatched with all regal velocity, reads, 'Whatever for?'

'Thus the enterprising but foolhardy pontifect was left with a bridge on his hands, since it was apparent to everyone that this newly-constructed thoroughfare, leading as it did from nowhere in particular to nowhere else at all, was a fumble. Occasional passers-by would point and mock, saying "Who's the bloody fool that build a bridge here? Ha ha ha!" "I don't know, must be wrong in the head," he would reply, puce with shame. For years he sat by the bridge, wearing a weak smile, until one autumn he was hit on the head by a Golden Delicious. "Eureka!" he barked evenly with a Job-like disregard for time and place. Then, in a daze, he made his second big mistake. Rather than building some decent restaurants, a couple of pubs, and a laundromat to attract human beings to his bridge, he hit on the rather dull idea of erecting some very high walls behind which a semi-aristocratic élite could hide from the outside world and go to each others' rooms for sherry. . . .' (An extract from Rev. E. Shepherd-Walwyn, *The Bridge Over the River Cam*, 1884.)

It is the year 1958. A Ford Anglia is juddering south along the A604, containing Chief Inspector and Mrs Chapman and a rather spotty figure, precociously dressed in the kind of suit that he thinks doctors might wear. He also has on a rugby club tie, and is busily reading *The Daily Telegraph*, trying to catch up on current affairs – a mistake he's never made since.[1] 'What,' he [I] thinks, 'will the Master of Emmanuel College ask me [him]?' His [my] headmaster has told me [him (me)] to let him, [not I (him)] do the talking, agree with him most of the time, but to disagree strongly on a few points to show that I [he, (that is me [I])] have one or two brain-cells. If he asks me any questions about English grammar I'll be up shit-creek. . . .

So I left two quivering parents, and attempted to saunter past a lot of very important-looking people in gowns, and stared round the courtyard. I could see no sign of a Master's Lodge. Overawed by the pauntly magnificence of the groups of overtly musing academics, I asked an old gardener where it was. He told me. I found the door, but I was a quarter of an hour early, so I walked around for a time, trying not to

1. This is no lie.

look conspicuous, and wondering why everyone was staring at me. At last it was four o'clock. I knocked on the door, and was greeted by the gardener, who asked me to come through to his study.

I said 'Yes' quite a lot, and nodded, particularly when he was talking about the history of coal-mining and the Industrial Revolution. But when asked whether I was going to pass my A-levels I gave a definite 'No' to Physics. He was clearly impressed by this and at last sensing a possible argument, thrust forward his head, raised his eyebrows to the point of nearly covering his bald patch, and asked, 'Why not?'

'Well, I'm not sure.'

'Not sure? Ah, that means you're in doubt?'

'Well . . . yes.'

'Do you mean yes?'

'. . . Er, yes.'

'So a pass is quite possible?'

'Yes, possible.'

'Probable even?'

'Well I . . . er . . .'

'Let me put it another way. Are you going to fail?'

'No.'

'Good, then we'll see you next October.'

I left, and stood for a moment in the corridor, trying to work out whether he had said 'yes' or 'no'. I decided that it amounted to an almost definite 'yes', walked back through the courtyard feeling that it was mine already, and was rather annoyed that no-one was staring at me.

'How did it go?' said the Anglia.

'Oh fine. Mind you, I've got to pass Physics.'

'Well, you'll do that,' it said, 'won't you?'

'Yes,' I replied confidently. The engine choked a few times, and then purred into motion.

'I think we've licked them this time,' said Flying Officer Edith, casting a victorious eye over the fast-disappearing Seat of Learning she had come to hate during her one-and-a-quarter-hour ordeal. Chief Inspector Biggles opened the throttle. He relaxed back into his seat with a satisfied grin, as the familiar drone of the 927 cc engine sped us on our way to eternity and sandwich-spread on toast.

A week later I was beginning to have my doubts. Could the man really have said 'yes'? Just like that? Would the rest of the college back up a gardener's judgement on my admission to Cambridge University? I was glad that while waiting for written confirmation I had been accepted by two London teaching hospitals – more realistic goals for a Melton Mowbray grammar-school oik.

At St Swithin's Hospital I had been submitted to twenty seconds of searching questions:

DEAN; Play rugby?

ME: Yes.

WARDEN: We've got a John Chapman here. Is he any relation of yours?

ME: He's my brother.

WARDEN: Right. See you in September.

DEAN: Wait a moment. What position d'you play?

ME: Second row.

DEAN: September it is, then.

St Mary's was if anything much tougher. I was seated in a room with a 110-page intelligence-test to be completed in fifteen minutes. An official started the clock and left me to it. After ten minutes I was still less than half way through and, as always in moments of panic, I thought, 'Steady on old man, you are English' and stopped. I lit my pipe and stared blankly at the clock for a whole minute, picked it up out of curiosity, toyed with it, and put it down again. *Somehow* or other, it seemed I now had another ten minutes to spare, which I thought I might as well spend completing their test. 'Hang on, aren't you cheating?' I asked myself. 'Yes, intelligently,' I replied. After lunch I returned for my interview. As I entered, the two interviewers flinched, because as far as they were concerned they were looking at a person with an I.Q. of 495. They blinked a little, nervously, and fell back onto the only line of questioning which they thought could outmanoeuvre Einstein and Bertrand Russell rolled into one:

DEAN: D'you play much sport?

ME: I'm very fond of mountaineering, but I've only led a few very severe climbs, and I'm not very experienced on snow and ice work. I play second row for Melton Mowbray Rugby Football Club First Team, and my brother is captain of the 'A' XV at Barts, though despite being six foot four inches tall I'm faster than him over 100 yards, having clocked 10·4 seconds at the age of fifteen-and-a-half, and I was second in the all-England Amateur Athletics Association 440-yard competition last year, the winner of which was Malcolm Yardley who equalled the European record of 40·1 seconds. I limped in a poor three seconds later, but it's not really my distance, and I only entered out of curiosity.

They apologized for not being able to think of any other questions, and said that unfortunately they would not be able to offer me a professorial chair for another seven years although it would be there for the asking if I could bear to wait that long. . . .

So by the end of the day I knew I could have a place at either St Swithin's or Mary's. I was still uncertain about Cambridge, but felt just sufficiently euphoric to join my brother later that evening at St Swithin's where he was holding his twenty-first birthday party.

When I arrived he was wearing a pin-stripe suit, a blood-coloured white shirt with a neatly stitched gash over his right eye and a bandaged right fist. The fist was the result of an assault he'd made on a fruit-machine in the Goat and Compasses. Apparently the rugby team had lost that day, and the thought of the fruit-machine beating him as well was too much. As the team were asked to leave the public house, someone decided it would be a good idea to climb into the coach and drive it through the window of a shop selling adding machines. Ten of the first XV found themselves in Casualty at their very own Regal and Historic Hospital, where a lot of very hushed-up stitching was done, and the unfortunate amateur-driver found himself several thousand pounds in debt. He is now a very successful and much respected doctor. I can't give his name but it is in fact Dr Charles Haughey.

All I remember about the party was that a rather large gentleman threw a pint pot at someone called McIlroy who had evidently not played awfully well. Fortunately he moved in time, and the pot embedded itself in the wall where his head had been. Affected by the relaxed atmosphere, I managed to persuade two others to help me throw painters' ladders and planks out of the fifth floor window, and we all watched the pleasant smashing effect they had on the railings beneath.

The next morning I woke up from a drunken coma to find myself inexplicably back in my bed in Melton Mowbray. I stumbled downstairs to breakfast. Perhaps yesterday's events had all been part of a drunken dream. But they couldn't have been. I definitely remembered my brother congratulating me on being accepted at St Swithin's. That was why I had drunk so much. . . .

I sat down to face breakfast with a spinning head and a mouth that could have been a British Rail ashtray. There was still no news from Cambridge. Suddenly there was a bellow from the direction of the front door of our house, which stood in the not particularly pauntly grounds of Melton Mowbray police station. My mother swept into the kitchen with a white envelope, gripped in the King George V Jubilee Commemoration zinc envelope-tongs. The jaws of the great tongs parted, and the envelope thffed onto the blue formica breakfast-table.

'It's from Cambridge,' she shrieked, feigning nonchalance.

'Kiss me Hardy,' I said, and broke the seal of my fate. . . .

I read the letter four times, looked out of the window for a moment, and read it again.

'What does it say,' said Edith.

'It says . . . it says . . . I think it says . . .' I went outside, walked around the house twice, and came back in to read the letter again. It had gone. There was nothing there . . . 'Oh well,' I thought. 'May as well finish my breakfast. You're mad, Chapman – we haven't got any zinc envelope-tongs, you were thinking of the Edward VIII Abdication mug which will be very valuable one day if we keep it long enough. . . .'

There were two matriarchal bellows in the distance accompanied by the yapping of handicapped corgis. I looked out of the window at the Assistant Chief Constable's house (naturally much grander than ours) and saw 'Shandy' dragging herself across the lawn – and though two under par in the leg department she was still very much a yapping concern. And there at the Assistant Chief Constablitic back door were And Mrs Chapman and And Mrs Ashcroft, resplendent in full evening dress about to commence their procession towards the big doors of the police station. There was a reverent hush from the crowd of non-commissioned officers and wives as the serene couple joined their husbands, wearing full Officers' Mess uniform, at the top of the big steps. As they paused briefly to acknowledge the crowd, cameras flashed and the *Leicester Tatler* caught the moment for posterity as:

Seen here enjoying a joke are (l. to r.) Assistant Chief Constable and Mrs Ashcroft and Chief Inspector and Mrs Chapman. Miss Jane Ashcroft (featured as Lay of the Month in our last issue) is expected to announce her engagement shortly to Mr Graham Chapman. Eyebrows have been raised in certain circles at this match, but Jane explained yesterday, 'We are very much in love. The fact that Graham has been accepted by Cambridge University has something at all to do with it.

I ran up, snatched the letter, dashed through the big doorway, grabbed a bunch of keys, ran upstairs, and locked myself in the snooker room. The letter was genuine. I had been accepted by Emmanuel College. But I decided with Darwin and Mendel that intra-constabulary breeding would be evolutionary folly. I had no wish to be sire to a brood of runted bluebottles.

Within four hours I had the Assistant Chief Constable on his knees outside the door, begging me to surrender this, the nerve-centre of his entire division. He agreed to my terms, the marriage was called off, and all two-hundred-and-sixteen copies of the *Leicester Tatler* were seized in a Midnight Suspected Porn Raid and spontaneously ignited while resisting arrest.

Calm was restored. Jane lived ever after, married to a man who looked like Sir Keith Joseph, and I ran away and hid for the entire summer, looking after a herd of goats in Cayton Bay.

I had passed all my A-levels and was very pleased to get 65% in Physics and an amazing 185% in Chemistry. Unfortunately I'd been taking the exams of the Oxford University Board, which were regarded with snotty-nosed contempt by the University of Cambridge. Apparently no-one knew anything about Chemistry in Oxford – they were all too busy lounging around in bottle-green velvet suits holding lilies and quoting lines by Tim Bryden and Denis Keat. This meant that I had to take a separate exam in Organic Chemistry.

And so I stood, facing a bench covered with apparatus I'd never seen before, in a vast brown hall. I wasn't alone. There were some forty other nervous candidates at similar benches, soiling their cavalry twills at the mind-boggling array of jars containing alien chemicals. Forty brains turned to dry ice as the invigilator stepped onto his podium and started the competition by saying, 'Gentlemen, you may now begin.' For ten minutes I tried to look as if I was doing something, moving bits of apparatus, taking the occasional apparently casual glance at the examination paper.

After eleven minutes of this useless activity I realized that I didn't know how to do a single experiment. For the first

time I experienced the full force of an attack of ignorance –
ears full of cotton wool, eyes staring into a tyro-blenching
void, legs that wouldn't move. Time seemed to stand still,
although a strange feeling in the nape of my buttocks told me
that it wasn't. . . .

Someone two benches away had apparently exploded, and
was being covered in an asbestos sheet by the invigilator and
two attendants.

came from behind me as a young gentleman from Hong
Kong ran for a fire-extinguisher. Then

as fragments of a Liebig condenser flew around the room like shrapnel. I now knew why they had brown walls in there. . . .

boomed the invigilator, 'Everybody stop! Right, if I find any more of you bloody idiots heating up ether over an open flame, I'll kill you. I haven't been a munitions expert in two world wars to get slaughtered by a load of ignorant tits. If you don't know what you're doing, get out.'

This didn't have a calming effect on anyone, but it did interrupt the trance-like state of the student opposite me, who began putting chemicals into a beaker. He measured out some pale blue liquid with confidence, added some white powder, poured in 5 cc of a colourless solution, placed it over a bunsen burner, and the contents of the beaker went a rather pleasing shade of orange. The man knew what he was doing, and I followed every move he made. I looked round to see what everyone else was doing, to double-check. After a series of manipulations we both finished up with a greyish powdery residue. From the wording of the question this should really have been white, but I was quite pleased at having any residue at all under the circumstances. However, my helpful friend wasn't satisfied with the impurity of his product. He must have the best. And reaching for the eth—

The next time I took the organic chemistry exam I was completely confident. Everyone appeared to be watching me. I was no longer frightened by the brown walls and the immense array of bottles and chemicals, and got a perfectly white crystalline substance. The same invigilator was present on his podium, and seemed much calmer, less imposing then the year before; he didn't even mind the odd **BANG!** I suspect his wife was no longer unfaithful, or that he'd had his piles removed.

I wasn't surprised that I passed. After all I was at Cambridge. I bought a gown, several club ties, walked around in a tweed suit with a pipe, and tried to look clever. The pipe was very useful because it meant that if anyone said anything

I didn't understand I could puff on it and seem incredibly deep in thought. The tweed suit didn't fool anybody, but the pipe worked a treat. In tutorials I was asked fewer questions; it also helped clobber the stench of formalin in the dissecting rooms. (This is one of the many hurdles in medicine. The first is dissecting a worm, a dog-fish and a rabbit at school. Then your very first real dead human being. I got over them, and within two weeks I was conveniently using my cadaver's mouth as an ashtray.)

The anatomy room attendant, whose name might as well be Wally, gave us all confidence by his matter-of-fact approach. He would sort through a whole box of limbs, heads and torsos looking for a nice one for you if you bought him a pint. 'Leg, wasn't it? Dear, dear!' he rummaged. 'They're a bit manky, sir. I can do you an arm and I'll keep back a nice leg for you next term. Now where are we? Arm, arm, arm, arm, ah yes here we are, a good one this. I thought it was in here somewhere.' And he pulled out an arm in an arm-sized plastic bag. It reeked of formalin, the preservative that Wally used to pump into the relatively fresh cadavers through the carotid artery before they were hung in a huge fridge by the ears. I asked him about the bits of meat and bone that he collected after they'd been dissected. How were they buried? And could he tell which bit was from which body? His reply was, 'Well, they're dead anyway, aren't they? The relatives don't know.' I immediately decided not to donate my body to medicine, but I have been asked by the General Medical Council to keep quiet about this bit.

As we all came to have the same sang-froid as Wally, we got used to the sight of spleens, gall bladders, the inside of the head and the nape of the neck. We became so used to our work that two people were sent down, one for using intestines as a skipping-rope, the other for frightening a young freshwoman medic who arrived home to find a severed penis in her handbag.

'A handbag?' exclaims Lady Windermere. 'I never said that! It was one of Lady Bracknell's.'

'Bull-sheeyit,' drawls Lady Bracknell. 'It's still you talking,

Oscar, honey chile. The witty ripostes are on you, remember. . . .'

But I can't remember, and as luck would have it more scenes from my past swim before my eyes. . . .

My first anatomy tutorial with the professor might well have gone badly if I hadn't been hiding behind a pipe. There were seven of us, all aged eighteen to nineteen. His first action was to ask the most innocent-looking member of the group to describe the breast. The poor lad could only make vague rotary gesturing motions with his hand and say, 'Well it's kind of hemispherical . . . sort of, er, er . . . sort of er, er . . .' and was ridiculed by the rest of the class. I laughed too, feeling secure behind my pipe. It soon became obvious to me that the Professor of Anatomy was obsessed by sex, and the fact that he had twenty-nine portraits of his family on his desk gave further proof.

At Professor Ferman's next tutorial, the same student, Hibben, was asked about the vagina. Everyone was giggling like schoolgirls (except me – I was still smoking my pipe).

'Describe the vagina, Hibben.'

'Er, right, well, it's a sensitive organ,' said Hibben.

'What d'you mean?' said the Professor.

'Well, it's about four and a half inches long and er . . . ah . . . is very sensitive.'

'Balls,' said the Professor. 'The only thing sensitive about the vagina is in front of it, lad, apart from a certain sensation because something has passed through the perineal musculature, the vagina itself is virtually numb. Your answer shows not only a lack of anatomical knowledge, but a complete social ignorance.' Hibben was too embarrassed even to go vermilion. 'You've obviously never slept with a woman,' said the Professor. Everyone giggled again, but Hibben pulled out a scalpel, slit the Professor's nostrils, gouged his eye out, cut his spleen with precision, and finished up by throwing the weapon into an autographed painting of his wife.

There was applause all round. 'I'm awfully sorry old chap,' said Hibben, 'but sex is rather a difficult subject. I don't know what came over me. Oh well, better go and

Sex is rather a difficult subject

have lunch I suppose – anyone coming to the Bunshop?' The Professor lay bleeding on the floor, and even in his last moments was dreaming of tits. The students filed out thinking 'Thank God that was a short tutorial,' and all of them, except the ones I'm going to mention later, lived happily ever after.

My tutor in physiology, Professor McKenna, was a Scotsman who now lives in Dunedin, New Zealand, so obviously you would use the word 'dour' in describing him. But it wouldn't be true. He was a tall, fat, randy bastard with a goatee beard with a very agile mind above it. Again at tutorials we all giggled at Hibben and the other four of us were rather glad that he took up so much of the Professor's time by questioning him, so he very rarely got round to discussing our essays.[1] After about five sessions Professor McKenna became irritated with our tittering, rounded on us and said, 'I like Hibben. Unlike the rest of you he knows how to ask the question "Why?", a habit that gets knocked out of us by parents at a very early age, when it should be a gift to be nurtured.'

We crept out with our notebooks full of humility. It was one of the few really important things I learned at Cambridge. But I still think I'd know more about the physiology of the human body than the urinary system if Hibben hadn't asked 'Why?' quite so often. Professor McKenna's little lecture had inspired him to ask 'Why?' at every possible occasion, and he often astounded ordinary passers-by by asking them 'Why?'

I wasn't aware that rabbits were capable of making any noise until I slit one's throat while it was nailed down in the physiology lab. I realized that the animal was technically dead in that its brain had been mushed up by a probe, and so could feel no pain. But I and my partner, James Wellwood, were a bit surprised when it raised its head from the block and squeaked. After a few puffs on our pipes we plucked up courage and slit its chest open, to find a rather disturbingly pulsating heart, which we courageously linked up to various

1. Essay: a collection of other people's thoughts disguised to look like one's own, in the judging of which originality is heavily penalized.

pieces of apparatus. Could this be vivisection? Yes,[1] we thought. But it soon all became fun.

Don't get me wrong, I'm not anti-vivisection. But I am anti-unnecessary vivisection. I've seen none of that in this country (UK), but I did see rather a lot of rats slaughtered at a medical school in New York where a newly-qualified intern was fiddling around with rats' brains without any apparent explanation for his action. He said he thought it was something to do with the pineal gland.[2] So what's a rat? They do the same thing with human beings there – with 'volunteer' prisoners – who, if they agree to have something alien inserted into their bodies – not just bits of plastic and metal but untried drugs – get reduced sentences. In this country, on the whole, we use medical students as guinea-pigs. I have never entered one of these contests, and I'm glad, because a friend of mine took part in a double-blind trial on a drug that brings down your blood pressure, only to find out a year later that it could cause permanent impotence. He was lucky to have been given the placebo.

1. The word 'Yes' remains in this text out of deference to democratic principles. Untrammelled by non-scientific co-authors I would have preferred the more accurate word 'No'. 'It cannot think, therefore it isn't.' Edith Descartes (Mlle.)

2. The pineal gland/body puzzles anatomists and physiologists to this day. It is now thought to have something to do with the production of, or control of, prostaglandins, ill-understood humoral agents (types of hormones, etc.) that have profound but inexplicable effects on our metabolism in all sorts of probably extremely important ways that are also ill-understood. Descartes insisted that the soul resided in the pineal body. Thinking that he could well have been right, I recently submitted an essay (rejected – *see* note 1 on page 68) to *The Lancet*, proposing that the pineal body could be the tax centre of the brain – a gland that sends out messenger substances into the bloodstream that call a halt to any form of work when the environment is unfavourable. Thus when a level of taxation approaching 83% is reached, the human body would fall into a state of inertia, all further activity seeming pointless.

Until the tax authorities are empowered surgically to remove the pineal gland the only treatment for this condition is by a financial operation whereby personal tax advisers force the sufferer to live in a more tax-beneficial but alien environment where productive work may be resumed. Very few of these operations are successful in that most patients find living without their family and friends and enemies, intolerable. Within one tax year they are reduced to drug-taking, madness or suicide.

The only experiment I've ever agreed to take part in was the inhalation of trilene – a mild anaesthetic that makes you feel 'phoo, phoo, baby' but then gives you a headache and makes you unable to eat pork pies in the Bunshop at lunchtime. One little test that I refused to be a subject in was the one where we were supposed to find each other's pain threshold. This consisted of occluding the blood-flow of the arm with a cuff and then soaking it alternately in hot and cold water. We were warned that the arterial blood-flow should not be occluded for more than half an hour, but that we should try to get up to that limit. Andrew Ransford, a six-foot eight South African, managed twenty-five minutes and a blue arm, so he couldn't eat pork pies either. But the pork pies didn't really matter since the next day I was banned from the Bunshop after one of my friends pissed on the fire, which was a pity because everyone – even I in those days – fancied the barmaid, and it was too hot in there.

In my first year at Cambridge I tried to join the Footlights Club, realizing that the only reason I'd gone there in the first place was that I'd seen Jonathan Miller performing in a television version of a Footlights annual revue. As a 'fresher' at the Societies Fair I went from stall to stall in my houndstooth-check, pork-pie hat and pipe. I didn't join CUCA, CuSoc, or Evangelical Aeromodelling, but did join the MedSoc, the Mountaineering Club, and other important political organizations. Eventually I arrived at my destination, the Footlights stall, behind which was David Frost, a lone figure boiling underpants. He told me that nobody could join since it was by invitation only. I questioned the point of the stall. 'None at all really,' said D. Paradine Frost. 'We only have twenty-five undergraduate members per year, so push off.'

I felt rejected and so paid £4 to join Acne Anonymous (Cambridge). I abided by the club rules and stayed in my room eating fresh vegetables for a whole year (24 weeks, Cantab.) apart from their Annual Dinner:

The President and Officers
of
Acne Anonymous (Cambridge)
Request the pleasure of . . . . 's Company
At La Pustule Au Jardin

On June 28th, Eight O'Clock Sharp

Yellow tie   RSVP The Hon Hugh de
                                              Chagspot-Pincenez (Cats.)

But I still hadn't been invited to join Footlights, the only purpose of my university career. Neither had Tony Branch, who had come to Cambridge to read Law, with the intention of switching to the Light Entertainment course after one term. We organized a smoking concert, or 'Smoker', a kind of cabaret-revue where people in dinner jackets and black ties sit around laughing at themselves – satire. I had invited the secretary of the Footlights, David Frost; the President of the Footlights, Peter Bellwood; Tim Brinton (a radio personality); Ngaio Marsh; the Gardener; D. H. and Frieda Lawrence; Lord David Cecil; Lord and Lady Clit; the Earl of Penis; and Sir Roger Lupin. We gave them gallons of claret, and didn't start until they'd drunk at least a bottle each. The show, just as we thought, was successful, and we were both invited to go to a Footlights audition before the committee, in the hope that they would allow us to appear in one of *their* smokers, which was a sort of sort of sort of second audition where you sort of sort of had to be awfully sort of funny.

I impersonated a carrot and a man with iron fingertips being pulled offstage by an enormous magnet. In the same set of auditions John Cleese did a routine of trampling on hamsters and can still do a good pain-ridden squeak. We were both selected and very soon were able to wear black taffeta sashes with '*Ars est celare artem*'[1] on them, as members of the committee, were able to prevent all sorts of talented people from joining the club.

The Footlights Club at that stage had had members the week before like Jimmy Edwards, Julian Salad, J. Miller, B. Gascoigne, The Goodles, Noel Coward, Irvin Thrush, Cole Porter (Honorary), Mr not Arthur Askey, Lesley Bricusse,

1. The art is to conceal the art.

71

and Tarquin Thing (who wrote all the Beatles hits and, pre-posthumously, curtsied at Muhammed Ali when he thought no-one was looking). Oh and also Peter Cook.

Although he'd by then 'gone down' from Cambridge, even in those days he had an obsessive disregard for David Frost, and came back to punish him by being funnier and more intelligent at the smoking concerts. I remember one particular sketch where Peter was talking as the Keeper of The Holy Bee of Ephesus, where he explained to the pilgrims that the Holy Bee was kept in a matchbox, but that it could cure all ills if they placed three shekels through the lid. After they'd given the three-shekel piece, and weren't cured of even one ill, he explained to them they'd probably stunned the Bee. Peter got rather angry with God during this routine, frequently cursing and pointing up to heaven because he'd had so many complaints from customers, and at one moment he went white and left the stage clutching his chest. Either he'd forgotten his lines, there was a God, or he'd overeaten.

But the most important thing about the Footlights Club was that it thought itself a more élite group than even the Footlights Club. The MCC had nothing on them. They wouldn't even allow HRH the Prince of Wales in to hoover the carpet. This taught all the members the kind of supreme arrogance that made Genghis Khan what he was yesterday.

But whatever the faults of the Footlights it was in fact more important than Cambridge University. Invisible to the outside world, but painfully obvious when you went for your first fitting, the University wore rose-coloured contact-lenses. All it could offer was three years of dull and pointless work, with no hope of a job at the end of it. While Footlights had a much more practical and enjoyable syllabus, ending with a very good chance of achieving what every human being really wants: fame.

The Footlights final examination took place over two weeks in June at the Cambridge Arts Theatre, and, if you earned a distinction, you would be offered postgraduate work at the Oxford Playhouse and the Traverse, Edinburgh; pick up a Ph.D. at the Lyric Theatre, Shaftesbury Avenue; followed by a lecture tour of New Zealand, and culminating in a Full Doctorate on Broadway. Our exams were open to public scrutiny, they were rigorous and cruelly fair. If you got laughs you passed – if not you failed. Compared to these, the university exams were about as reliable a guide to a student's ability as the width of his mother's kneecaps, and I treated them with the nonchalance they deserved.

Around me others were going mad with the terror of failure. The strain was too much for one gentleman on my staircase whom the head porter found throwing his own shit about the room. He made a hell of a mess of the place and was carried off screaming. I think he got an *aegrotat*, which means that he got his degree but didn't have to take the exam because of illness.

Two other aegrotats were less genuine. One law student, who had done no work at all except on bottles of claret, hired a car and had himself driven out into the middle of the Fens, where he was found a week later, wandering around in the fields, claiming that he had amnesia. In case he's forgotten again, his name is . . . but then I'm sure he hasn't.

Another friend, who was reading Oriental Studies, had spent his three years at Cambridge flying aeroplanes. He faked appendicitis, and because his two main papers were several days apart, was brave, stupid or afraid enough to be slit up and have the perfectly healthy organ removed.

I left Cambridge with a BA in Natural Sciences (lower second class), several bottles of the College sherry, and a PhD in Claret. I returned for a short time to Melton Mowbray and looked forward to seeing my old schoolfriends on the traditional Friday night in the Bell Hotel. . . . Why was I looking forward to it? The last time I'd seen them they'd become irremediably dull. They were all getting married and settling down and unable to come out for more than half a pint, and their only escape from their wives was to talk constantly about cars – was the TR3 better than the TR2; how are Lotus doing this year; bloody gasket went last week, twenty-five quid down the drain, well you've got to think of the labour; oh you should have done it yourself – it only took me twelve days; ah but you were on holiday . . . I butted in and asked, 'What's happening to Marlene these days?' 'Changed her name to Jane – teaching I think – she's got some clapped-out MG. . . .'

'D'you want another round?' I asked, having bought the first and only round so far, and having waited impatiently for the past hour for someone else to cough up.

'No thanks, we've all got to go back and not communicate with our wives.'

'Hey, there's the Spanish Grand Prix on the goggle box tonight!' said someone else.

'Oh right then, must be off, can't miss that.' And they ran off into their three-up, one-and-a-half down rabbit holes with garages and wives that resembled sacks of flour in print frocks, who had all done courses in Domestic Science, which taught them how to make sponge cakes, drop-scones and strawberry gateau, and how to become dextrous enough to do the ironing while stroking the cat. To be fair to them, in Domestic Science they were taught that all food comes out of tins or frozen packages. The English educational system, as far as food is concerned, even now maintains that you practically have to have a Nobel Prize in Cuisine to produce food without the taste of lard. Even the English aristocracy give themselves the title 'Lord', which is merely a corruption of the word 'lard', as in 'He's well larded', 'lardy-da', etc.[1]

So why was I going to see these friends? Well, quite honestly, to brag. About how I'd just performed at the Edinburgh Festival. And chatted to Lawrence Durrell and another man in a dirty raincoat called Henry Miller. And how we'd been round to lunch at Lady Craythorne's, with Lord David Cecil and Anthony Asquith, or 'Puffin' as we called him. And how Dame Edith Evans had – but I was already at the door of the Bell. I paused briefly in the entrance to thumb through Chapter One of my *vade-mecum*, *Niven's Book of Names*[2], then strode confidently in. There was no one there.

---

1. *From Teach Yourself Wit* by M. Muggeridge and Betty Pules (Miss), authors of *I Will Teach You After Dinner Speaking*, and *1001 Jokes About Bladders*, with a foreword by Ring Larder, author of *999½ Jokes About Breasts And Buttocks*.

2. More than just a guide to casual name-dropping, this invaluable handbook is a gold-mine for those seeking self-enhancement by proxy. So personal are the details that they are beyond verification – even, I suspect by the celebrities themselves. I very much doubt for instance whether Richard Burton remembers the night he spent with Clint Eastwood, let alone what is supposed to have ensued. Two minutes ago I didn't believe it myself but even as I dictate this I am putting on my coat to nip up the pub and tell Dennis. Vroom!

The barmaid explained that some of my friends had been in earlier.

I looked at my watch. It was only five past nine. Premature domesticity had struck again.

The only person I knew in the bar was Peter Cox, a thirty-four-year-old solicitor and secretary of the Rugby Club. I joined him. He had already bought a pint and a whisky chaser for me. Within twelve seconds it was my round – 'same again Doris'. Halfway through the next pint we paused to greet each other.

'Ah, that's better,' he said. 'Good to see you. Same again Doris.' And while we were waiting for the next round he apologized for the delay in ordering the drinks. 'Sorry about that. Must be that blasted honeymoon.'

'What?'

'Just driven up from Heathrow, had to drop Jane back at the house on the way. Nearly made me late for opening time!'

Pleasantly unaffected by marriage, he continued, 'Liked your Footlights Show at the Edinburgh Festival – you're not going to carry on with medicine now are you?'

'Yes I am.'

'Not for long, though.'

'Well . . .'

'Thought not.'

'Ah well, I . . .'

'You ought to do the show in the West End . . . Bloody drab place, Melton Mowbray – never come back here again. I mean what do your mates do now, talk about cars and babies and what a good time they used to have at school? Get out there, and for Christ's sake enjoy it – that's what life's for.'

He gesticulated with his hook at Doris. 'Same again please, and a bag of nuts for the parrot. Now Graham, lad, we'll see if we can't give you the kind of send-off as the likes of them two-bdm.-one-recep.-k/dinette-gas-c.h.-small-gdn.-lubbers'll remember till the Quorn Hunt meets in Penang. . . . Be you in 'ere this next Friday afore the first pint is drawn. . . . There's enough o'talking now, there be only one and a 'alf hour's drinkin' left afore I go back to that accursed wife o' mine.'

A week later I had just collected a round from the bar during a lull which was almost detectable in the dull conversation. 'A half for Jane, half-pint for Paul, a babycham for you, Jane, a half for Tony, and an orange juice and packet of crisps for Jane, a babycham and a half of lager and lime for Jane and Robbo, and that's Tim's half. Tim are you sure Jane won't have anything?'

'No thanks, she's driving.'

Roars of laughter at this dazzling off-the-cuff remark. I sat down and started the first of the three pints I had bought for myself. Paul started the ball rolling with 'You should have been in here last week, Graham.'

'Why, what happened?'

'David Pratt came in here with Patricia Clayton's dog.'

'Patricia Clayton?'

'You remember, used to be called Jane.'

'Oh.'

'Anyway, in walks David with this corgi, and quick as a flash Robbo says, "Got you walking the dog now, has she?"'

Two giggling Janes were unable to control their mirth any longer, and splattered the table with a Melton Mowbray version of Buck's Fizz.

'Stop it, Jane,' said Paul. 'The boss's wife comes in here. Evening Mrs Warrilow. Chilly isn't it? Stop it, Jane.'

Handkerchiefs were passed. Was this the Paul who three years ago had driven his father's Vauxhall backwards at 70 m.p.h. through a stone wall?

'I'm off to London tonight,' I said.

'Oh, you'll be going on the A606 to Stamford then?' said Tony.

'No,' said Robbo authoritatively, 'you want the A607 to Leicester, then it's a straight run on the A426 to the start of the M1 at Lutterworth.'

'Ah but then you have the Leicester traffic at this time of night on a Friday,' said Paul. 'You'd be better cutting through to Marston Trussell on the B4036 and picking up the M1 south of Northampton.'

The double doors of the lounge bar were flung open. Two trumpeters split the air with Duke Ellington's 'Hydrogen Wedding Anniversary Stomp', heralding the arrival of the

The cuckoo leaves its nest

magnificent early Georgian sedan-chair. I recognized it instantly as one the First XV had stolen during their raid on Cheltenham Ladies' College, but, by their amazement, I could see that no-one else did. All four Janes gaped as I stepped into it, and was carried out into the hotel courtyard. The entire bar followed me out, glasses in hand, and watched as the Master of the Quorn Hunt assisted me from the sedan-chair to the rear door of the waiting Rolls Royce Silver Cloud. The driver turned round, rubbed a conspiratorial hook on the side of his nose, and we glode off, keeping the setting sun well to the west of us.

And that, Best Beloved, is how the Cuckoo left its Nest.

CHAPTER FOUR

St Swithin's

In September 1962 the reconditioned engine of the Ford Anglia purred out of action in front of College Hall, St Swithin's Hospital Medical School. I ordered Chapman, my father, to carry my trunk up to my room, and went to a nearby inn while he and his wife unpacked my belongings and tidied up the room for my arrival. I left the pub at 3.30, walked back through the courtyard past a lot of rather spotty ex-grammar school boys – absolute oiks the lot of them – strolled up to my room, and dismissed my parents. I cast my eyes around the room – the bed looked too narrow. I tested it for creakiness and made a mental note to tell the porter to bring me a larger and less creaky place to sleep. On the desk – a bakelite version of bird's-eye maple – I noticed something wrapped in greaseproof paper[1]. I unwrapped the package. It was a cake from my mother 'How sweet,' I thought, as I threw it into the waste paper basket.

I opened a small suitcase containing my books: *Climbing in*

1. A piece of paper soaked in lard.

Snowdonia, Nanga Parbat, The Ascent of K2, Cambridge University in the Andes, The Art of Coarse Rugby, and *I'll Teach You Drinking*. I flicked through a few pages of this volume and came to St Swithin's Hospital. It had three stars by it.

The most important feature of those three years of clinical study was the bar.[1]

I learned all of my medicine drinking at it. Unfortunately its ability to teach Surgery and Midwifery was inadequate, and I consequently failed in both subjects. This meant that I had to spend a gruelling six months doing cabaret in a night club and writing for David Frost. This gave me sufficient arrogance to pass them both easily. I should really have learned that lesson months before, when someone whose name I conveniently forget, who had spent his three clinical years playing bridge and poker, passed his finals without ever having examined a patient. All medicine is a gamble, and he was extremely good at it, having stripped at least a dozen students of their grants.

But that's all so much hot air under the bridge. Let us return to the most important aspects of medical training. The bar had been run by a layperson, it was open only between six and seven in the evening, and it ran at a huge loss. Fingers were being dipped into tills, and the occasional large scotches went missing. Stephen Carter, who was Chairman of the Students Union at the time, thought it would be a good idea if his twin brother, Stephen Jenkins, formed what is now

---

1. This is all fiction including the name 'St Swithin's'. Otherwise the names have been kept the same, only the facts altered; this to fit in with the tradition begun by the doyen of medical writers, Richard Gordon, whose real name is Gordon Ostlere, who, incidentally, actually wrote an extremely good medical textbook, *Anaesthetics for Medical Students* which contains the only truly funny line in any of the huge tomes that are a medical student's obligatory unfunny reading. The centenary edition of *Gray's Anatomy*, for instance, clocked up 1604 pages of smirkless facts, Cecil and Loeb's *Textbook of Medicine* amounts to nearly 2000 titterless pages. Bailey and Love's 1308-page 1975 edition of their curiously titled *Short Practice of Surgery* is no laugh-a-page pamphlet, although Fig. 1156, representing the rectal impalement of a suitably clad English Country Gentleman on his shooting stick is a quick giggle, closely followed by their Fig. 1157, 'Pepperpot in Rectum'. A radiograph showing a pepperpot in the rectum was later found to be inscribed 'A present from Margate'.

called the Hippocras Society, and we took the whole thing over, running it with voluntary student labour.

Within a year we were beginning to make almost embarrassing profits, and decided that these should be spent to the benefit of the Students Union. However, not everyone in the Students Union drank – some were even Christian Union. We thought that a selected list of people who spent most money at the bar should be the ones to benefit most. Democracy was in progress. We put up a list of some thirty people's signatures, leaving only two blank spaces for those students who would like to visit a Moët et Chandon château in Rheims, a day trip costing each member a mere £5 for the flight, the rest of the fare being subsidized by the Hippocras Society. This notice was appropriately pinned up in the bar, and, as expected, the remaining two places were not filled by people from the Christian Union. The plan was working. Count Moët was given the definite impression that his château was being visited by thirty-two consultants from Harley Street. We assembled at the bar at 6 o'clock in the morning and had a breakfast of lager, climbed on to a coach containing crates of lager, and left for Brighton Airport.

We all arrived at Rheims with extremely high blood-alcohol levels, and were given champagne by the Count himself. He seemed to be quite pleased that we weren't a load of stuffy consultants. We had a magnificent three-hour lunch in the Orangerie, and tried to keep the bread-throwing to a minimum and throwing-up at least discreet. The Count was enjoying himself, and he ordered jeroboams of his 1911 Champagne. People on the top table were determined to get the pilot pissed, and they succeeded. He left, thinking of his immediate future of piloting, to rest for a few hours.

We then went on a tour of the cellars. The vast barrels, which probably still have 'St Swithin's for the Cup' written on them, impressed us very quickly. The rest of the tour, being dry, was completed as speedily as possible. Leaving the chateau we went back into the town of Rheims, a quiet place with something called a cathedral in it, which we glanced at from a bar. Outside the bar was a large papier-mâché effigy of a Moët et Chandon champagne bottle, which a certain person, whose name I conveniently forget, thought would look nice on the Hippocras Society's bar top. We arranged things so that he would commit the actual theft while the rest of us drove round the square at high speed in the coach, grabbing it at the last moment. We drove round the square and found Benson (sorry Benson) who hadn't realized that the bottle was chained to the wall of the bar, arguing with a shopkeeper and a gendarme about the tremendous benefit to Moët et Chandon that a trophy like this would bring them in terms of English advertising. The policeman was clearly unimpressed, but Benson, while continuing his line of argument, turned round, threw up, and talked on as though nothing had happened. The natives were completely thrown by his aplomb, and although we didn't get the bottle we were allowed to carry on to the airport.

At Rheims airport, they wouldn't let us leave the coach because the driver had lost his jacket and identity papers, and for some reason thought that a certain person in the coach might be responsible. We waited for Benson to own up, and then were allowed to board the plane. During the flight I remember a different certain person, who is now a consultant paediatrician, hanging from the luggage rack, trouserless, chanting 'Eskimo Nell'. The single air hostess, who was at first a little embarrassed at having to pass under his crutch to reach the front of the plane, must have complained to the pilot. We were all so happy that we filled in the time, (those of us who could stand) by standing at the front of the plane, jumping on the spot, then running down to the other end and doing the same thing in the hope that we could tip the thing up. We nearly succeeded and were told that the police would be waiting for us at Brighton.

The responsible members of the group, that is the Hippocras Society, who were used to drinking, picked people up off the floor and strapped them into their seats before landing. As we landed, we could see that the appropriate reception bay was rather filled by people in dark blue pointed helmets, so, as the plane was taxi-ing in, we all leapt out before it had stopped and ran in through another bay. The police greeted an empty plane, while we rushed through the gate into Customs. A fight nearly broke out with the officials, which we would certainly have won in the short-term.

Someone called Benson wasn't wearing trousers, and no-one would own up to having hidden them. He explained with confidence that shirt-tails was his national dress, pointing to Alistair McMaster who being a very Scottish person also had no trousery substances. The culprit owned up quickly, thinking of the policemen behind us, and we were allowed through on to the coach, with its engine already revving and several Stella lagers already open.

It was an uneventful journey back until we reached St Paul's Cathedral, where one of the Carter-Jenkins twins, either the one who had his hair parted on the left or the one that had it parted on the right (which was Stephen), was pushed out of the coach wearing nothing except a bowler hat. He found an *Evening Standard* from a nearby stall, and confidently walked through the city, covering his genitals with the newspaper, to the Medical College. Well, it was dark, he was wearing a bowler hat, and it was the Evening Standard, so no-one noticed, and he arrived at the College, fully nude, ten minutes later.

Something in my soul told me that this was Medicine.

To supplement my meagre student grant I decided to do some cabaret. Full of confidence, being ex-Footlights, Tony Hendra and myself went along to the Blue Angel nightclub for an audition. We chose the Blue Angel because it was one of the best nightclub spots for revue and we'd read in *The Stage* – in an advertisement that sounded like whistling in the dark – how David Frost had recently been retained there for a 'second glorious month'. However, we were accepted at the audition and in two weeks' time found ourselves top of the bill, which meant we didn't start our act until any time from two to two-thirty a.m., meaning that I didn't get back to College until three-thirty, having to get up again at eight-thirty in time for a ward round at nine. I found this routine too gruelling after five more weeks and we left the Blue Angel, to be followed by a promising newcomer called Dave Allen.

We found a more lucrative and conveniently timed engagement at Edmundo Ros's Club though artistically this was less successful, in that the patrons were more interested in the hostesses than two funny guys. My two most immediate

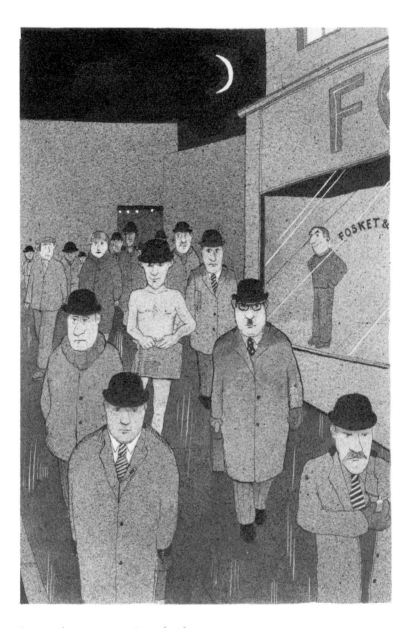

It was the Evening Standard

recollections of that particular club are of Coca Cola costing the equivalent of two pounds a bottle and a 'hostess' returning after an intimate tête-à-tête to tell her friend, 'Look at this, the bloody fool's gone and given me a diamond ring.' I looked at the poor, fat, sad businessman as he scurried out. . . .

On another occasion at the Blue Angel a drunken guards officer – they formed about fifteen per cent of the clientele – who was annoying us and the rest of the audience by his untimely and incomprehensible interruptions eventually clambered up on to the stage so Tony Hendra took a swing at him and knocked him out cold. We carried on with our act to thunderous applause from the audience.

All this helped to provide me with money to buy mountaineering equipment for brief weekends in the Peak District and holidays in Scotland and, of course a more ample supply of loot for the bar. Later when things were getting a bit tight, I joined the cast of the revue *Cambridge Circus* when they moved from the Arts Theatre to the Lyric, Shaftesbury Avenue – but more of that revue later on.

But I wasn't just at St Swithin's Hospital to perform latenight cabarets and West End revues, I also helped to start annual concerts for the Hippocras Society and organize the Christmas 'Ward Shows'. The last was a splendid excuse for avoiding a family Christmas. I could join in with the rest of the lads wandering round the wards, entertaining the moribund with liberal supplies of barrels of beer made portable by the use of hospital trolleys. Some of the nursing staff, the huge matron in particular, raised objections to these festive revels in that they were disruptive of hospital routine and in certain cases where beds were trampled on by spectators – deleterious to the well-being of patients, but if I were ill enough to need to be in hospital over Christmas I can think of no better atmosphere in which to peg out: nurses wearing silly hats, urine bottles decorated with holly, mistletoe on the drip stands, general bacchanalia.

Apart from entertainment there was yet another side to medicine.

I was used to dead bodies, but I now had to deal with live human beings. This was another hurdle to overcome, and I remember on my first day as a 'dresser' we were taught by the houseman how to take blood from patients. He suggested that we should all take blood from each other, and lined us up in pairs, so that you would take 5 ml of blood from your partner, who would then take 5 ml of blood from you. Fortunately he left, and we were on our own. I refused to have my blood taken by the idiot who was my partner, and I'm sure he felt the same about me.

I arrived alone at the ward the next morning at 8.30 to find that I had to take what amounted to about a pint of blood from nine different patients. And so I practised on them. I only missed a few veins, and by the end of the morning was getting quite good at it. And, as everyone knows in a hospital, if you complain you get worse treatment, less attention, and an ice-cold enema.

The next couple of weeks I spent pretending to look like a doctor while looking at people's faeces and staring into their sputum jars. There was one particular patient whom the nurses had finally refused to bath.

His abdominal surgery had been mismanaged at another hospital and he'd been brought into the teaching hospital to be sorted out. His abdomen had been covered with aluminium paste in an attempt to prevent the excoriation of the skin caused by his five substitute arseholes. It was as though his bowels had been doctored by a telephone engineer. Any competent plumber would have done a better job. No-one really knew which hole led where. Marcus Pine and myself, as dressers, were ordered by the Sister to bath him. We put him into a bath which we filled with disinfectant, and were both vaguely nauseated by the unformed turds which slipped out of his orifices. He was pleased by the comfort of the bath and the fact that we hadn't thrown up in his presence. We dried him, carried him back to bed, and he died the next morning.

There was an incident which struck a not-too-distant relative of the Archbishop of Canterbury, His Grace the Mind-Bogglingly Reverend Something – she was called Rachel Fisher (a very attractive female student with large breasts and long flowing dark hair and deep brown eyes that would have put even a minor canon off his muesli) – who was a senior dresser on my ward, and quite unable to finish sentences properly . . . (I mean she could finish sentences, obviously, otherwise she'd still be talking . . . d'you think this is a reasonable place to stop?) . . . bother, I've forgotten where I was now . . . anyway (what a terrible word – what does it mean? It means nothing, like 'actually' and 'in fact' and 'sort of' . . . it's a . . . kind of . . . well, basically it's ah . . . the product of a hesitant mind) . . . anyway, Rachel Fisher, who was then a good friend of and is now married to Dr Alan Bailey, remarked (he recalls), 'We had a new student on the ward-round the other day, knew fuck-all about medicine, but he was very funny . . .'

I remember that ward-round. When asked to describe the physical signs in a patient's abdomen by an impressive consultant surgeon, affectionately referred to as 'the Beast', I offered the product of a hesitant mind and said, 'Well, there were no abdominal signs, in fact.'

The Beast asked, 'What do you mean, "in fact"?'

'I meant as opposed to fiction, sir.'

Which, I suppose, is what Rachel meant. . . .

Ward rounds were designed to instruct the students, make consultants look impressive and frighten the patients. To the patients a consultant was 'the specialist', a direct descendant of Aesculapius, a living god who rarely made contact with mortals. And ward sisters liked it that way. Over in the medical wards, Sister Goderich, who had spent most of her morning chivvying nurses and patients into making her ward impeccable for the professor's ward-round, returned to ask her staff nurse how the ward-round had gone. Staff Nurse said, 'Very well, Sister, but . . .'

'Nurse, what on earth are those screens still doing round that bed?' yelled Sister. 'Remove them at once, it's time for the patient's lunch . . .'

Staff Nurse gallantly attempted another 'But . . .'

Too late, Sister had already charged over and drawn aside the offending curtains revealing an unexpected tableau of His Dignity, the Professor-of-Medicine, washing a youth's hair. This incident could be viewed as contrary to the tender-loving-care-between-medically-and-non-medically-qualified-consenting-adults-only-Act. Questions were asked.

This led to scenes of angry parents confronting the Board

of Governors. I found this whole incident morally repugnant. What did people like that think they were doing? A clear example of abuse of position. By the parents. If I had my way those parents would be put inside and sanctimonious sisters shot. Fortunately the Board of Governors was not composed of closet-dykes and the whole matter was seen in its proper perspective.

John Cleese, who had just finished his finals in Cambridge, getting a rather snooty upper second, wanted somewhere to stay in London while he wrote for BBC Radio such things as *Yule Be Surprised*, a Christmas show for Dick Emery. I was very friendly with the junior warden, Buzz Mangrove, and had managed to find a pass key to all of the rooms in the hall of residence (on the black market), and I knew that there were several empty ones. I gave John the key and suggested that he should stay in the room normally occupied by a person called Nick Spratt. Now Nick Spratt was a direct but distant descendant of Sir Percival Spratt, the first surgeon to really be a surgeon rather than a barber.

I first met Nick in Cambridge when he was President of the Mountaineering Club and I knew that he was at that time away as the doctor on an expedition in Greenland. He was a very athletic person who always entered the inter-hospitals London to Brighton walk. In his final year at St Swithin's he was doing a locum but decided rather than miss the walk he would run the whole way there and back, returning at 8 o'clock in the morning for his clinic. He arrived at 6.30 in time for a cup of coffee and a bacon sandwich after having made the kind of run that would make Roger Bannister look wet. He was the embodiment of the spirit of England – courageous, kind and stupid.[1] He said 'yup' when a 'yes' would have done.

On the Greenland expedition Nick had an accident. He was leading the climb up to a peak and while roped up to the rest of the party fell through a thin layer of snow covering a crevasse. The rope stopped his fall about sixty feet down and his only reaction was to call to his second, saying, 'Oh, um, are you all right?' His second dragged him out of the crevasse

1. Used here in the sense of having concealed wisdom.

88

and he returned to England rather sooner than he expected to find his room filled with a sleeping John Cleese. But, being a gentleman, he came in and said, 'Oh, um, yup . . . er, sorry!' and went out, and slept the rest of the night in the bath.

Buzz Mangrove, a gentleman too, mentioned to me that perhaps Mr Cleese should begin to think of finding alternative accommodation. Buzz at this time was five foot one, and I've no reason to believe that he's grown any bigger now. And apart from being junior warden at the hostel, he was senior registrar to the man called the Beast (*vide supra*). The Beast was senior surgeon and stood six foot and five inches with no shoes and excluding bright red hair, which meant that Buzz during operations had to stand on a box. The Beast would do anything – he was the last of the heroic surgeons. He would inspire such confidence in his ability that patients would practically plead to have their entire livers taken out by him. I remember one day most particularly when the Beast was operating and he told Buzz that he had a malignant melanoma (an extremely nasty kind of cancer) on his own big toe. He climbed up on to the table and asked Buzz to amputate it. Buzz didn't want to do this, but the Beast insisted he was right. The toe was removed and the report came back from Pathology reading 'Blood blister'.

Buzz also had a problem in that a student who had arrived from Oxford, and was known by everyone as 'TCP', because of his habit of bathing in the stuff, was a fetishist in cleanliness. Bathing in neat TCP four times a day[1] had given him a bright red phenol rash all over his body, and you could smell him four hundred yards away. People in the lift used to remark, 'What's that strange smell?' when they were on Floor 2, even though TCP lived three floors above that. Huge bottles of TCP could be found outside his door, and in the bathroom he even had TCP toothpaste. He was the cleanest man in existence, but not the healthiest.

Unfortunately for him, as a student on his first day in the theatre, he was supposed to be assisting Buzz Mangrove and the Beast. The Beast, having shown off in front of a lot of visiting Greek surgeons, had marched out of the theatre,

1. Definitely not recommended by the makers.

leaving Buzz to sew up. Poor TCP, who should have been there an hour and a half earlier, wasn't. Not because he'd been late arriving at the operating theatre, but merely because his scrubbing-up procedure was so meticulous that it took him half an hour rather than the recommended five minutes. He was so preoccupied with his fear of germs that he shook a great deal each time he came into the theatre, and so desterilized himself on the X-Ray machines, anaesthetic apparatus, and bits of the wall. Each time he was sent off by the theatre sister to scrub up again. The Beast had gone, but before Buzz sewed up the patient he thought he would show TCP what the Beast had done. He opened up the retractors so that TCP could get a good view of the fine surgery that had been performed – a portacaval anastomosis. TCP looked into the gaping abdomen and PLOP! his spectacles fell right into the middle of the wound. Buzz and the rest of the theatre staff had hysterics – while poor TCP, whose spectacles must have been cleaner than anyone else's in the world, was carried out by two porters for psychiatric therapy.

The consultant anaesthetist at St Swithin's was a splendid character called James Grimsdyke. He was the original Grimsdyke in Richard Gordon's 'Doctor' books, and they were contemporary students for a time.

An extremely rich aunt had left him in her will £1000 annually until such time as he qualified. He had sussed out the unintended possibilities of this codicil and spent thirteen years not qualifying. He ran a pack of hounds and a bridge school, never appeared at lectures, and made sure that none of his experiments went well. Unfortunately, World War II caught up with him. In 1939 they'd pass anybody, and because he'd taken the course in anaesthetics more than anyone else in history, he was immediately made consultant anaesthetist in East India Command. He was a great success.

He came back later as consultant anaesthetist at St Swithin's. His carefully studied, but apparently cavalier, approach to life made him a celebrity. Patients loved him because of the confidence he inspired; surgeons loved him because patients under his care didn't bleed. He was adept at keeping a patient's blood pressure at what more timid anaesthetists would think dangerousishly low levels. (He had condensed Guedel's five stages and two hundred planes of anaesthesia to three: (1) Awake; (2) Asleep; (3) Dead.) James was a stylist, a skilled craftsman and a gentleman physician, and to the students one of the most approachable consultants.

It was my turn to do a month of anaesthetics. Alistair McMaster, a huge but squat Scot, and I were assigned to James to be trained in the art of putting people to sleep. The night before we started was the Rugby Club Dinner, and we all had a very good time in one of the few places from which we weren't banned. I was supposed to be in the theatre with James at eight the next morning. I woke at 8.30, puked, and ran over to the hospital.

Alistair was already there and looking a bit white as he wheeled his patient into the theatre. I apologized for my lateness. James said, 'Don't worry, dear boy, you can do the next one – Alistair'll show you,' and went off to read *Autocar* in the Surgeons Only. After the operation Alistair came out. I'd been frantically reading *Anaesthetics for Medical Students* by Gordon Ostlere (see page 80), and asked Alistair what the hell I should do when the next patient came in. He explained. It seemed simple enough. He was looking happier and rather proud at having given his first anaesthetic. I gained some of his confidence and some of James's. 'The man must trust me,' I thought. 'I'd better not get anything wrong.' And after all, if anything did go wrong, James would be just around the corner.

I injected exactly the right amount of Brietal and Suxemethonium, stuffed a tube down the patient's throat, wheeled him proudly into the theatre, and connected him to the gas machine. Halfway through the complicated abdominal operation, my patient started to twitch. The surgeon eyed me suspiciously. I turned up the CO_2, having read in the book that this would help clear up hiccoughs. It did. The crisis was over and I was fully in control of the situation. I humbly suggested that the surgeon could continue. Then the patient gave an enormous jack-knife type jerk, and the surgeon politely asked me what the fuck was going on. I left Alistair with the gas machine and went to find James, expecting him to rush out and save the day. I found him reading *The West Country Beagling Gazette* over a cup of coffee and a cucumber sandwich. 'The patient seems to be getting a bit light, sir,' I said.

'Deepen him, dear boy, deepen him.'

The logic was inescapable. I went back, turned the valve up another notch, and there were no more complaints from surgeon or patient.

One of James's greatest achievements, both socially and as an anaesthetist, was to formulate a new kind of punch:

Dr J. Grimsdyke, MD, FFARCS
St Swithin's Hospital
London

For Mr. H. Society

R̸ 2 bottles red wine   31 Dec 1962

2 bottles white wine

325 mls of martini

1 bottle dark rum

½ lb honey

1 pt lapsang Souchong tea
strained into the heated mixture

to be taken P.R.N.   mitte 2 Gallons

It is a very elegant preparation, an excellent piece of pharmacy. The alcohol is there for obvious reasons – a simple anaesthetic. The honey disguises the strength of the mixture and helps it slip down a treat. The caffeine in the tea makes everyone think they aren't getting drunk, and after two pints of medicine they fall over, go to sleep, and wake up temporarily blind. The efficacy of *Elixir Jacobus Grimsdaecii* can be verified by several testimonials:

'Better than Dr Collis Browne's' *H. Nilsson*

'I banged my floor on the head with joy' *Tim Brooke-Taylor*

'Shgreat . . . Waagh! Oh, sorry about the flower-bed, old man' *Alan Bailey*

'For Christ's sake someone help me up' *Alan Bailey*

'Who turned the lights out?' *Alan Bailey*

1. Where ⟨⟩ is to be revealed in Volume VIII.

CAUTION: *There is no known antidote to this preparation. General supportive measures and gastric lavage offer the only hope of recovery.*

A month later I was a student in the Ear Nose and Throat Department. One morning I remember the Registrar arriving after the Boat Club Dinner, looking green and fragile. It was one of our jobs to clean out regularly the smelly scabs and unpleasant excretions from patients who had been treated for chronic hay-fever, sinusitis, etc. by having their nasal mucosa burnt out. I had finished probing around with my forceps inside the nostrils of a pleasant old lady and had in my kidney-dish a rather rewarding yield of scaly yellow bits. Next to me the Registrar was attempting to look down a patient's throat. I placed my dish on the table between us and my patient left happily with a note to return four weeks later. Then while looking at the back of a patient's throat through a dental mirror the Registrar glanced sideways and noticed the pus-encrusted scrapings. His patient gagged as though about to vomit, but the Registrar got in first and threw up all over him.

My sexual life at St Swithins consisted of going to bed with women while dreaming about men. (This is hardly even partly true in retrospect. It's just that I definitely do remember, once or twice, thoughts of men's bodies creeping into my mind while in coitus, only that sort of thing just doesn't make for neat sentences.) The first one was the student's traditional friend, a nurse, a sack of flour that you met at a hop and persuaded back to your room for coffee, having put all the chairs in a friend's room so that the only seating accommodation is the bed. She was rather podgy and extremely repellent, but I just wanted to get my end away. She must have been some kind of descendant of Richard Gordon's 'Rigor Mortis' – perhaps her mother was a nurse at St Swithin's in about 1939. She was a real 'lie down, think of hockey and England' type, and after a brief grope that was not enthusiastically received I thought, 'The bar's still open, I'll get rid of her.' She said, 'It's too late now. Matron says we must be in by 10.30.' Was this some kind of devious come-on? I looked her hard in the breasts and thought 'Yuk'. I politely pushed her out of the room, across the square to the hospital, and over the traditional nurses' hostel entrance, the mortuary gate. Then I ran back to the bar.

The second was an old school friend called Sonia Burrows, whom for the purposes of this book I shall call Sonia Burrows. I tried like hell to get into that one, only to be obstructed by a tampon, anorexia nervosa, and vaginismus.

I was twenty-four, still a virgin in terms of women, and desperate to try the whole thing out. Nothing succeeds like excess, said Ozzie Wilde, and so one day in the refectory I sat down nearest the most attractive female student I could find, and asked her out to dinner. There was some confusion. I didn't realize that she was almost totally deaf, which must have made her a bit of a hazard with a stethoscope in later life.

There was another female student. We had noticed each other across tables filled with lard-sodden meals. She was getting a lot of attention from the lads but of a rather fawning, not-daring-to-ask nature. It was 'Can I carry your books home?' time. . . . She was drooled over constantly. With very good legs, small but well-formed tits, she was at least as intelligent as Alexis de Tocqueville, Alexander Graham Bell and Alec Plitt put in a box. And so, on an idyllic summer afternoon – it was tea-time in the students' refectory – I sat down at her table. Ignoring her minions I boldly passed her a plate of sandwich-spread sandwiches and asked her if she'd 'go'.

She was intelligent enough to say, 'See you in my room tonight', with none of this pointless preamble of going out to dinner, sitting in cinemas holding sweaty hands, love letters, and all that timid avoidance of the real issue. We had a bloody good time for a whole year. She was athletic and imaginative. We went right through the card. It wasn't just British Missionary, but doggie, on the floor, on the floor standing, on her desk, in the shower, in the bath, near the bath, at someone else's place while they weren't looking, and in a guard's van through the whole of Birmingham. I liked the experience, but after about nine months or so it began to pall, and I felt I would rather spend more time in the bar drinking with the lads, hoping to be too late back in my room for the, 'Hello, I'm lonesome' telephone call.

'See you in my room tonight'

For a bit of variation one night I tried the wife of a student who'd been foolish enough to get married. She had about three children then, but she was still raring to go. She had large knockers and a very thorough knowledge of what dongs like. Her husband was a friend of Buzz Mangrove and was pissed out of his mind in the bar, but Buzz had noticed her absence, and suspected me. He didn't interrupt but listened outside my door as I came (between her breasts) for the second time . . . The description of this passage has made me feel so . . . uh . . . uhm . . . ah . . . ah . . . excuse me. . . .

After all this frenzied activity I decided that I should do some clinical test on myself, so whenever I went in a taxi-cab, tube, train or bus, I looked at each passer-by and tried to tell myself honestly which ones I would like to go to bed with. And the ratio of boys to girls was something like 7:3, which puts me clearly on the homosexual side of the scale as suggested in the Kinsey report.[4] I was largely homosexual and worried about it. A trip to New Zealand and America made me a little more broad-minded about myself, and immediately after qualifying I gave up medicine and became a raging poof[5]. But no mincing – a butch one with a pipe.

There are a lot more memories of St Swithin's Hospital, and I'd like to fill up a bit of paper with them. There were several interesting exhibits in the Pathology Museum. One was a live 25 mm shell from an aircraft gun. It had been found by the hospital up the anus of a squadron leader who was in the habit of pushing back his piles with it. He had been rather enthusiastic in his method of treatment one day, lost his grip on the thing, and finished up with the unexploded missile in his sigmoid colon. The entire theatre staff wore air-raid helmets for the operation.

I may as well carry on with a few more perineal anecdotes. I remember one gentleman who claimed to have had an accident in his bathroom in that he had the bad luck to sit down

4. Not only the number of this footnote but also about my rating on the Kinsey scale, ✹ being exclusively heterosexual; ⊞ exclusively homosexual and 4 meaning: predominantly homosexual but more than incidentally heterosexual.

5. Medical men are not all scientists, which could be why they overlook the possibility of free individual choice in their weird quest for a 'cause' for homosexuality.

on an upturned cigar-tube. No-one believed him. But it was a damn sight easier to remove than the milk bottle that found its way past the anal sphincter of a middle-aged gentleman from Reading. The problem was overcome rather neatly, a plastic catheter was inserted and guided into the top of the bottle, which was then filled with plaster of paris. The theatre staff went off for tea while it set. The bottle was then turned round, as an obstetrician would turn a breach, and yanked out on the end of the catheter. This patient was unusual in that most people with this kind of complaint come from a prison where things are so bleeding boring that there's really nothing to do except stuff things up your arse.

Moving on to the anterior part of the perineum we come, in males, to the penis. I remember two gentlemen who both arrived at Casualty wearing raincoats. They both refused to tell the hospital porter what was wrong with them, and he explained that if they didn't tell him he couldn't send them to the right department. They refused to speak to anyone but a doctor. . . . He correctly assumed that it was something sexual, and because the venerologist wasn't around, sent them to Casualty. One of them had, on examination, a curtain ring and the finger-hole of a pair of scissors surrounding the base of his penis. He claimed that his wife had put them there one night when he was drunk because he'd been unfaithful. The brass ring was sawn through relatively easily, but it took three hours and four Gigli saws to cut through the stainless steel scissors.

The other embarrassed gentleman opened his coat to my brother, a house surgeon at the time, to reveal a milk bottle that had somehow slipped over his dong. It was complaining, understandably, by swelling up. The usual remedies – injections of hyaluronadase and applications of cold lard – were tried, but it wouldn't move. So my brother arranged a suture trolley, wrapped a towel round the bottle neck, and hit it with a hammer. The bottle broke, miraculously without leaving a mark.

The 408th anniversay of the abdication of King Charles V of Spain, that is the 16th of January 1964, was a cold, depressing day. The Vietnam war was in full swing, President Kennedy was barely two months dead, and I thought it might be just as well to go and have a few pints in the Cow and Calf. I met several friends in the bar, and after a lot of pints Benson led us in a few verses of 'The Farmer's Boy', complete with obscene gestures. He did the best turkey I have ever seen, and a ram that would have rated with the finest, standing on a bar-stool. The landlady complained at the point where he was demonstrating cowpats. He explained to her that she was a whore and that her husband didn't know about the number of men *he* knew she'd been with, then carried on singing. She fled to find her husband, the landlord. The singing continued. A window was smashed accidentally by someone who felt like throwing a pint glass. When the landlord was brave enough to complain, he was removed from behind the bar and locked in the Ladies. We carried on singing, but the police soon arrived to spoil the day and see the whole of St Swithin's Hospital barred from the Cow and Calf. Even members of the Christian Union were refused orange juices and told to get out after that.

The police took us round to the Police Station, where we were questioned as to whether we would like a drink and a game of snooker. We stayed for several of both, and about time too – they'd used our table five times in the last month without even buying a round.

Even as a student member of the medical profession you are in a privileged position. I remember an evening when a grand piano was caused to be thrown out of a fourth floor window in the resident surgeons' quarters. The police arrived and were greeted with a barrage of water bombs, that is rubber finger-stalls (as used in anal examinations) and contraceptives filled with water. It was agreed that all the damage would be paid for, and we all went back to our place for a drink, where we ran around in their helmets making strange mooing noises, while McIndoe, who had already completed a zumba,[1] was streaking round the college lawn in the snow, nude, lit by the headlamps of the Dean's Morris Minor which happened to be in a tree at the time.

The same week, the Carter-Jenkins twins decided that they

1. A strange ritual in which a male person who has made an error in the verse of a song takes off his clothes in time to a repetitive chant from his colleagues.

didn't like Peter Redwing because he didn't like their friend Chris Brinton. After a few nights listening to Peter Redwing's pathetic attempts at sex, they rigged up some microphones, recorded his efforts and played back the tape to the lads the next morning. Then they hit on the idea of bringing him out into the open. They very carefully arranged all the furniture and belongings from his room in the middle of the lawn in the snow. Peter arrived back in time to find them still on the lawn arranging his 'room', and say, 'Hey, chaps, what's going on?' Without pausing, they explained that they'd just taken everything out of Chris Brinton's room and put it on the lawn. Peter Redwing thought this was very funny. He leapt on to the bed and pissed all over it, kicked in a few pieces of furniture, including a gramophone, and went back to his surprisingly empty room.

As a medical student at that time you were required to drag out at least twenty babies on your own, and sew up the results of your errors. I went to St Clives Hospital in South London for four weeks, and my fellow student there was called David Sadza. We shared a room. He, through no fault of God's, happened to be black, and I white. The staff nurse in midwifery (I blame God for this) happened to be South African and very white. So David did about four deliveries to my forty. He was quite simply never asked, because blacks could not be trusted. He was not even allowed to do the sewing up after an episiotomy.[1]

I became quite good at sewing up vaginas, I suppose because I was thinking of their past and future contents. But I was rather annoyed that, while a new regulation had just come into force, allowing midwives to do episiotomies, so that they were keen to do one whenever they could, they were not allowed to do stitching, so students like G. Chapman were disturbed every half hour to repair their messy work – which meant that I kept missing David Frost's *Not So Much A Programme More A Way Of Life*.

There was a patient I once examined just before the programme, I thought she was in labour and likely to give birth soon. The South African midwife, who had already accused

1. That is, cutting through the labia and perineal musculature to ease the passage of the probably unwanted infant into a life it didn't ask for.

me of losing the keys to the drug cupboard, said, 'No, she isn't. She's only fourteen and hasn't got any pains.' I informed her that pains, and her age for that matter, were quite irrelevant, and that all the signs, including the contractions, showed that she was definitely in the first stage of labour. The midwife said 'Nonsense' and I went back to watch the programme. Just as Bernard Levin was about to say something very interesting to Harvey Orkin I got bleeped, ran up to the labour ward, and while I was scrubbing up the girl gave birth. The midwives panicked. I gave the girl her child after the formality of tying off the umbilical cord and weighing the placenta. She asked me my name, and, in gratitude, called the placenta 'Graham', though the child had to be called 'Alvar' after its father.

It was the easiest birth I have ever seen, perhaps because she was so young and had none of the fear and worry that is commonly induced by older members of the female sex in order to dramatize their role in life. I have always thought of birth as one of the most natural processes and one not needing the interference of medical science. Most women in the world have their babies behind a bush in a squatting position, in which even a breach delivery can be performed by one person without unnatural interference. For male readers: imagine being nine months constipated having inadvertently swallowed a coconut whole, and then being asked to lie on an operating table, legs apart, with lots of people watching dressed in silly clothes. Would you be able to shit? In my view, maternity wards should consist of carefully arranged shrubberies, with earplugs for each mother so they don't have to hear, 'Ooh, I had a terrible time with my first'; 'Wrong way round is it dear?'; 'Oh poor thing, twenty-five stitches I had the last time'; and 'They've got you on a drip, have they?' Childbirth would be completely painless if grandmothers had their lips sewn up.

And if anyone ever says to you, 'I didn't go through all that agony to bring you into the world for this', either (1) run away; (2) punch them in the teeth; or (3) say, 'Don't give me that, you fucking cow; if you want to go and work in a pit hacking out fucking coal all day, you bloody well can.'

I got fed up with having to sew up so many unnecessary

incisions, and annoyed at the South African staff nurse's attitude towards my friend. One night, after I had just finished
sewing up a patient, he was called to a delivery. The South
African nurse refused to allow him into the theatre, and I was
called. I arrived to find a perfectly natural birth in progress,
and was told by the South African nurse that Mr Sadza had
refused to do an episiotomy. I said that I agreed with him,
there didn't seem to be any need for one, but the harridan
kept advancing with a pair of scissors. I said, 'No, this one's
all right.' The baby's head had already stretched the vagina
and it seemed obvious that it would come out without help
or damage to the mother. She insisted that it wouldn't, and
again approached the labia with her scissors. I hit her on the
jaw with my elbow and she fell to the floor. (I was keeping
my hands sterile for the delivery of an intact baby.) The baby
was born from an unscathed vagina. This was as much a
relief to me as to the mother; the medico-legal complications
of a split perineum combined with an assaulted midwife,
would not have been pauntly in the least.

CHAPTER FIVE

New Zealand

March 1964. The new Biochemistry and Physiology Block of St Swithin's Hospital was being opened by Her Majesty the Queen Mother. At the time, being Secretary of the Students' Union, I was invited to join Her Majesty for tea with other representatives of the student body after her tour of the new premises. The Queen Mother had an excellent complexion and was extremely charming. I was very pleased to find out that she had asked to come to tea with the students and not with a lot of old gits in red gowns and stupid floppy hats.

During tea I explained to Her Majesty that I'd had the offer of going to New Zealand as a member of the cast of *Cambridge Circus*, a revue, but that this would mean taking six months off medicine, and my parents had yelped strongly against this. The Royal Person said, 'It's a beautiful place, you must go.' I used this remark on my parents as if it were a royal command, and it worked. My mother was now able to go into the butcher's shop and say, 'Oh, the Queen Mother said he must go.'

Ten minutes later[1] I was on a plane to Christchurch. John Cleese had a shower in Karachi, lost his watch, and held up the plane for an hour while he looked for it. I didn't particularly mind the delay, because I was sitting next to a rather nice-looking Commonwealth sailor.

We arrived at Sydney at 'sivun tin' and took the next plane for Christchurch at 'twilve twunty'. Christchurch was a shit-hole of a place, made all the worse because we'd left England in Spring and arrived there in Autumn. It was pissing down rain, and cold. We were taken to a temperance hotel made of wood. After an appalling meal we were shown to our rooms. Mine was so cold and damp that there was mildew on the bed-covers. To try and warm the room up I turned on the hot water tap and lit a small bonfire in my ashtray. The next morning we all complained about the damp and cold, and demanded hot water bottles for the next night.

Breakfast was served from eight to nine in the morning in a damp room the size of a moist barn. We all gathered together at one table only to be told that we had to sit at a table which was appropriate to our room number or we would not be served. That meant that the nine of us sat at separate tables dotted around the room. There were only two other residents. We shouted at each other across the room, saying that if things didn't improve we'd move out.

I looked at the menu. The first course was 'Porridge or cremona'. I asked the waitress what cremona was and she said 'Porridge'. Hardly believing this, I looked at the second course which was 'Fruit or prunes'. I asked what the fruit was, and she said 'Prunes'. That night we all arrived back from rehearsal to find hot-water bottles in our beds. Unfortunately they leaked, which may have encouraged the mildew, but not us. We left.

The whole group moved to a hotel built of brick that served drinks to the residents. (You have to bear in mind that the licensing laws in New Zealand at that time meant that bars could open only between 5.30 and 6.00 pm. This meant, of course, that at 6.10 pm the streets were full of white New

1. Roughly.

Zealanders beating up Maoris, or the other way round, depending on who had managed to get the most drunk quickest.) We felt very privileged at the access to drink and warm beds, and slept quite happily until noon the next day.

John Cleese and myself decided to have lunch at the hotel because we were performing in the theatre that afternoon and evening, and it didn't seem likely that we would get a meal. I asked for a three-egg omelette. The waitress was astonished, and said, 'What?' I said, 'A three-egg omelette' and pointed to the words on the menu saying 'three-egg omelette'. She said, 'A three-igg omlut?' and I said 'Yis', pointing again. Five minutes later she returned with a large omelette with three fried eggs on top. Even people three tables away threw up.

We flew to Dunedin, a town in the south of the island, named after a mixture of Edinburgh and Dundee, and with a perceptible Scottish influence. We stayed at a hotel called the Leviathan (where breakfast was served from eight to five past eight) completely uncontaminated by alcohol or women. I even had a tartan tooth-mug; and the surrounding country-side had the nerve to look just like Scotland. But I did see, in one glen, an animal resembling an orange to russet furry pig. John Cleese flatly refused to believe this description, so I put the whole incident down to alcohol withdrawal symptoms.

Tim Brooke-Taylor and I got desperate. We asked the stage-hands if there was anywhere we could get a drink after the show. After a lot of chatting we convinced them that we weren't the police, and they told us that there was one place, but that we had to knock three times and ask for Jock. After the show we arrived, knocked three times, a little shutter in the door opened, and we asked for Jock. From the far side of the door we could hear the unmistakable sound of glasses being hidden. Tim asked, 'Is Jock there?' We were told that he could be, but what ship were we from. I suppose there has always been an affinity between the navy and 'theatrical people', but I can't think what it is. We explained that we were from SS His Majesty's Theatre, and were allowed in. And provided that we bought an orange juice or coca-cola, they would give us a pint of lager each on the strict understanding that we should hide it if there was another knock on the door. There was a knock on the door. Everyone in the room hid their lagers and stood drinking orange juice as the police walked round. They had a quick scotch with the barman and left, satisfied with our temperance.

I learned later that the temperance societies in New Zealand were largely financed by the breweries, and that the reason for this was that if the licensing laws were extended they would have to spend more money on pubs and staff to run them. They made a better profit the other way, out of off-sale bottled beer and spirits.

We flew to Timaru, a town about the size of my house – the only difference being that there is no seafront in Highgate and Timaru doesn't have a theatre as big as mine. We arrived with our costumes, props, and lipstick, walking down the aisle of an auditorium that held a paltry 2000, to find Humphrey Barclay, a producer not commonly known to be related to a bank. He was setting up the lighting for the evening's performance which was particularly important because it was being recorded for New Zealand Television, an organization slightly bigger than the New Zealand Navy. He was shouting at the electricians for more light. They turned all the available stage lighting up to full. He screamed at them again that this was not good enough. The cast by now was on stage, arranging props and doing a walk-through. None of us could quite understand the need for extra lighting in that we were already being blinded by the fierce glare from every part of the theatre. Humphrey, now in a frenzy, foamed at the nostrils and roared for more light. He threw off his sunglasses in anger, realized he'd been wearing them, sat down, and went puce.

I wanted to see the mountains, the New Zealand Alps, and managed to persuade John Cleese and Tim Brooke-Taylor to join me in paying for a flight around them. It was a spiffing flight, with heavenly views that really gripped you by the balls – well actually the bit between your balls and your arsehole – they were Great with a capital 'G', one 'r', one 'e', an 'a' and a 't' (in lower case). The single-prop four-seater Cessna's engine purred as Captain W. E. Hillary flew us across mountain ridges, emerald green chasms in the ice, and countless glaciers. We landed on one of the glaciers that had been counted.

'Crikey!' whistled Ginger Brooke-Taylor. 'Damn good thing old Groupy put the skis on the old underbelly!'

'Yes. Eeuuurp!' confided John 'Algy' Cleese into his air-sickness bag as we came in to land on the Fox Glacier. Tim and I stepped out of the plane, exhilarated and confident, and sank into four feet of snow. Apart from that nothing happened. Group Captain W. G. Grace taxied the 'plane round for take-off, the engine revved, and the Cessna shot off for all the world like a gannet into the blue with bits of white.

We yelled and stamped so much with indignation that we sank another foot into the snow and, as luck would have it, thereby attracted the attention of Sir Edmund Hillary and Uffa Fox who had been playing poker for several months in their marooned Ford Anglia while waiting for the snow to thaw. At first they were alarmed at our intrustion. They wanted to be alone together. The atmosphere was tense.

'Excuse me, ahem, ahem, can you tell me the way to Timaru?' I volunteered.

They tried to cover up their embarrassment with small talk as they rearranged their clothing. 'Just have a look at that gearbox,' as zips were zipped and duvet jackets velcroed. Eventually the newly-clothed pair made us a delightful tea of cucumber sandwiches with drop-scones and clotted cream. They apologized for the lack of honey, and we had three charming months of witty small-talk as we glid genteelly down the mountainside to Timaru.

In Wellington, the capital city, we did what amounted to a Royal Command Performance, since Sir Bernard Ferguson, the Governor General, was coming to see the show. The entire audience had to stand until he arrived and the national anthem had finished. As soon as he sat down so could everyone else. He told us later that he'd once unfortunately been twenty minutes late in appearing, that the entire audience stood to attention the whole time, listening to the national anthem played nine times through. They still hadn't realized that they weren't part of an empire.

Auckland is a larger town than Wellington, and there is even one building you could describe as a restaurant. Their most splendid nightclub, boasting fine views over the South Pacific, and called 'The South Pacific', did overlook the South Pacific. But verisimilitude ended there. We did a cabaret there in exchange for a free meal and drink. The waitresses were startled when we asked if we could possibly have some rolls to go with our soup. We then tried 'bread' or 'toast', and after a lot of uneasy consultation they eventually came up to the table with a half-empty packet of stale pre-sliced loaf. The rest of the meal was worse.

So little happens in New Zealand. They had just had a visit from The Beatles, so entertainment from England was *the* thing. And being the young cast of a popular show we were followed everywhere by keen fans. Mine was Mike Cormack, a handsome eighteen-year-old student. He showed me round the town in a car borrowed from his parents, and took four of us to his father's batch[1] near Lake Taupo. I liked him, but I didn't know I was gay, and I don't think he knew he was. And so I missed out on my first real opportunity, when there were just two of us together, looking out on a view of Auckland Harbour, a beautiful sunset, and a gents bog.

I suppose the fear of labelling myself homosexual held me back. There was certainly no-one to watch us, and I was 12,000 miles from my father's binoculars. Mike, I'm sure – he has written to me since – was even more keen to get his rocks off. But parental sexual repression and a bigoted government and social climate (probably influenced by the bad food) meant that the two of us stood there, quivering, neither wanting to make the first move. I pretended to have a pee, we exchanged some comments about the lack of bulbs in the light-fittings, and drove back in silence to Auckland.

'What a bloody fucking waste of time,' I thought three years later when I was in Ibiza, hugging David in a tent, feeling more liberated and happy than ever before in my life. I realized then that I didn't have to have women all the time, and that guilt is the weapon used by a muddled society to stop people having a good time. 'All the world loves a lover.' What crap! Even in the sexually liberated 'seventies young people still had to get pissed or high to do what they really wanted to do in the first place.

1. Weekend retreat.

My own strategy then in the fight against guilt was to go out and do what I felt guilty of again and again, and again the next morning if I felt like it – an anti-aversion therapy therapy, but this meant a liver-boggling amount of drinking.

On the way from Auckland to Hong Kong, we stopped off for a few days in Sydney, which compared with any city in New Zealand seems like Gomorrah . . . or was it Sodom? No it wasn't, bugger it.

John, Tim and I were met in Hong Kong by a rich doctor's widow, whose son, Benny Chi Ping Lee, had trained with me in the bar at St Swithin's. We were treated extremely well, with exceptional food cooked by the authentic Chinese-type Chinese maid, and with a lackey who would pick up the dog for anyone who felt like stroking it. We didn't use this service very often as it was an extremely fierce dog. Mrs Lee took us to the best hotels for cocktails, and to lantern-lit floating restaurants with really fresh fish swimming in cages over the side. You pointed out the one you either liked or hated and it would be killed in any way you wished. I had one of my fish killed in a white wine and green ginger sauce, although it was the stuffing of finely chopped scallions, fried almonds and lemon juice that really finished it off. John Cleese's fish was so fresh he had to batter it over the head with an empty sake bottle before it would agree to go down his throat. We restricted ourselves to twenty-nine more courses and seven bottles of strawberry liqueur, and then, as on most evenings, we would travel round the town in rickshaws, abusing the natives, popping into nightclubs for a swiftie, don't you know, what!, then off to the Hilton where we sat for dinner on leather-lined air-conditioned commodes overlooking the authentically squalid sampans in Kowloon harbour, just like the ones on the British Airways[1] pamphlet.

On our last day we were allowed to roam the streets a little on our own while Mrs Lee went shopping, and we soon noticed that ninety-nine point nine per cent of the population weren't spiffingly rich. In fact three million of them were living on tiny boats as big as a medium-sized cucumber frame, with tattered linoleum instead of glass. A few of the sampans, with untattered roofs, were owned by the Chinese

1. *Née* B.O.A.C.

equivalent of the middle class. These families had become 'wealthy' by selling their bodily orifices to foreign tourists. And when I was showing an 8 mm film of *Visit to Hong Kong* by G. Chapman, I found it rather difficult to explain to my mother what all those little children were doing backing towards me patting their bottoms.

It was our last day in Hong Kong, fuck it, and that's what Tim and I decided we should do. While John was buying another camera we explained to Mrs Lee that we had to post some letters and would meet her back outside the camera shop in a 'few minutes'. We ran off down the street and found the Japanese massage parlour that we'd both not noticed earlier. We ran up the stairs to find ourselves in front of a door with a tiny spy-hole in it. Tim wanted to run away, so did I, but being foolish I pressed the bell. Someone looked at us. Tim was by now giggling with fear, and the thought that he might have his prick rubbed. 'Bring bring bring!' went the bell, because they always do in stupid lying narratives like this. The door opened. 'Creak creak,' it went, again as they always do, and we both rather staggered at the sight of a Japanese-style Chinese girl wearing a kimono and a bottle of scent. We both fainted. But the heavy scent and the over-whelming hint of sex soon roused us. Tim was taken off to have a Turkish bath, and I was taken in to be massaged.

I wasn't exactly sure how many clothes to take off while the young lady was out of the room, but on balance thought that all was a good idea. And I lay back downwards on the couch with a small towel over the naughty bits. The perform-ance started. First the oil, scented with secret balms, was rubbed into my flesh. I was caressed and beautifully pom-melled, followed by an application of some form of talcum powder, and then stroked with such ambidexterous erotic fluency that I thought I'd even embarrass myself. She paid no attention to anything I could muster, and I was wondering if I should grab her and force my by now obvious intentions on her. But then I was English, and I only wondered. She said, 'Turn over.' I didn't quite know what to expect at this point but I obliged. She left the booth, and I wondered for a moment as to what she would come back with. She didn't. A young Chinese gentleman came in and gave my back a right pasting, culminating in him walking up and down both sides of my spine. Absolute bloody agony. But I didn't dare cry out as I knew Tim would hear me.

Eventually the torture was finished, and I went through to the Turkish bath, passing Tim on the way. We both gave indications that we were enjoying things tremendously, and while in the bath I waited to hear Tim's screams when the man walked all over his back. He didn't scream. Damn the British. I left the bath and was asked by the young lady whether I would like to be assisted in my shower. I replied automatically, 'Oh, no, quite all right, thank you. Oh. Wait a minute. Um. Well, perhaps.' Too late. She had taken me literally.

Tim and I left feeling radiant – well, not radiant, horny really. I found out that he had also refused 'assistance'. We both regretted that we were English. We had to rush back to meet Mrs Lee, but quite honestly I could have fucked a letter-box. As opposed to fiction, I wanked three times within an hour of the plane leaving Hong Kong.

After my tour of New Zealand and three months in New York with *Cambridge Circus* (*vide supra et infra*) I came back to St Swithin's to pass Pathology and Therapeutics extremely well, narrowly missing one of the two 'prizes' in Therapeutics – well, at least, I was in the last six. Then came my final exams: Medicine, Surgery, Midwifery and Gynaecology. Medicine I felt I didn't deserve to pass but did; realizing how little you know is the first step towards. . . .

Surgery I should have passed but didn't. I knew that I'd passed on my paper and my short cases were simple enough; a row of about ten patients you have to diagnose quickly and suggest possible treatment for, and for my long case I had an extremely cooperative patient who told me much more than she should have about her thyrotoxicosis and its surgical treatment. Unfortunately for me a rather silly man, a pompous surgeon, wearing a scarlet gown and a silly floppy hat for the sole purpose of intimidating examinees, asked me where I'd been trained. He took exception to the fact that it was St Swithin's and in particular had great personal animosity towards the Beast. I failed.

Midwifery I felt I should have passed, but did rather mess

up my long case, never having encountered a pregnant dwarf, with unusual hip deformities as a result of a road accident, during any of my tuition, even in any text-book small print.

This meant that I had six months to spend before I could take the examinations again. I didn't need to do a great deal of work on Surgery, just to keep my revision topped up. I read for about an hour a day and went to the occasional ward rounds. My tutor in Gynaecology and Midwifery was so enraged at my failure that he gave me a third degree grilling in his weekly tutorials that I attended. This left the rest of my time free to write with John Cleese and go to script-conferences for *The Frost Report*, a programme featuring D. Paradine Frost, J. Cleese, R. Barker and R. Corbett.

My introduction to fellow-writers Michael Palin, Terry Jones, Eric Idle, Barry Cryer, Dick Vosburgh, David Nobbs, etc. was a very happy one and at the end of a very successful run of thirteen half-hour programmes I had no problem with Midwifery and Gynaecology and passed quite easily. Surgery too, seemed to be easier this time with the exception of an extremely uncooperative patient for my long case, a fat lump of a man of forty-five years of age whose only complaint was painful ankles, and a mild, chronic bronchitis. This could have been arthritis because of his obese condition but that just wasn't enough to discuss for my main case. I started again, asking him about his weight; whether he had lost or gained any recently. 'No,' he insisted he hadn't, his weight had *remained* the same for years. After a complete re-examination I'd nothing to add to my findings and the prospect of failure loomed as I approached the Professor of Surgery. I told him what I'd found, he agreed and simply said, 'And?'

'Well, and that's all, sir.'

'Did you ask him about his weight?'

'Yes, sir, he said it's been the same for years.'

'Did he? Are you sure you asked him about his weight?'

For some reason my confidence returned. I didn't want to go through all this again. 'Yes, I asked him several times. *He said it had stayed the same.*'

'I don't think so,' added another examiner at the Professor's side.

'*Well go and ask him!*' I almost shouted.

This they did and came back and the professor said somewhat apologetically, 'What *would* you have thought if he had told you that he had lost two stones in weight in the last month?'

'Cancer, sir!'

'Where of?'

'Lung, sir.'

'Look at those X-rays.' I did. There was the growth. This man had been selected as a difficult 'long case', purely because the only indicative symptoms were recent weight loss accompanied by swollen ankles – a variant of peripheral pulmonary arthropathy, commonly seen in the fingers, but then only recently described as a diagnostic sign in the ankle.

After this I happily went through the suggested courses of treatment and the prognosis for the patient. They were pleased. I passed. I was pleased.

CHAPTER SIX

Ibiza

After my final examinations the prospect of three months writing a film on a Mediterranean island appealed to me more than six months of looking into ears, noses and throats.

The new long-fuselage Boeing Ford Anglia log. 7³√987 GTQ stopped. Its engines didn't choke, splutter or cough, the wheels did not screech on the tarmac, and the nearest aeroplane that actually shuddered to a halt was a Douglas Dakota (Prototype) at Reykjavik on January 8th 1937. Neither did the grim-faced pilot throw off his goggles, sigh with relief, turn to his co-pilot and say, 'We made it Ginger.'

But none of this stopped the air-hostess doing her bit over the tannoy: 'On behalf of Captain Morpeth and the Muir of Ord we hope you have had a pleasant flight. Would you please remain seated until the irrational and claustrophobic grappling around the two exits has come to a complete halt. I don't know about you, but this is definitely my last flight with Air Faecal Pellets, and the reason is that I have now spent three years staggering up and down between rows of cramped seats filled with conceited American businessmen grabbing my arse – though God knows why, because they couldn't even fuck their own fists on alternate Fridays – wearing this humiliating priapic costume – where's the so-called "glamour" in that? Even the pilot – who I happen to know is being fucked by a policeman in Benidorm – is hardly likely to come and give me a twatful of God's own juice, which I gather is so good for the teeth. And there's no point in any of you tittering like that – it goes without saying that all of you will have to wait three quarters of an hour in the plane at 110°F, then pour out into an airport bus which will drive you three times round the plane and then zig-zag the twenty yards to the corrugated iron Arrivals Hutch, where you will have to wait another three quarters of an hour at 120° for the privilege of having your passport messily stamped by a myopic, unshaven bureaucrat in Woolworth's "Dago" reflecting sunglasses. While you are standing there you will see Captain "Clint" Morpeth and his co-pilot who thinks he's James Bond (you can tell him by his red face, a stench of Japanese body-rub, and the time-expired packet of Durex in his top pocket) streak through hours ahead of anyone else clutching their contraband, which will be very annoying for you, 'cause by then you'll be dying for a piss and there's absolutely nowhere for you to go. Even then you'll have to face the baggage claim with the suitcase that goes round and round for forty minutes looking like yours, and *if* you get your luggage, it'll be grabbed by some petty-bourgeois bum-biter of a customs officer who thinks he's General Franco 'cause he's got two stripes round his sleeve, who will force it open at the hinges and sweat torrentially all over your fresh white cotton shirts in search of smuggled dried lizards and illicit pinball machines. Finally you'll get out and there'll be no buses to the town so you'll have to take a taxi and be charged £35 for a two-mile ride on burning plastic seats that scald your . . . Oh you'll never learn, will you? Just get off.' Click.

After I had checked out of the airport I was met by Loretta Feldman, who called herself 'Mary O'Sullivan' on a forged passport. She took me to a car driven by her husband, called

Marty. On the way back from the airport we chatted happily about how appalling D. Frost was, and arrived at a restaurant called the Green Dolphin. Inside the Green Dolphin were John Cleese with some tart,[1] Marty, his wife, Tim Brooke-Taylor, and several pictures of Nazi war criminals. Because we were supposed to be taking the ladies out I was paying double for something I didn't get. I didn't mind too much – I was drunk, and, needing a piss, I went into the Gents. I noticed that the soap above the sink was stuck on a prong and looked curiously like a half-erect penis, even though most of it was green. I rejoined the table and Tim Brooke-Taylor was ready to micturate. I explained to him that there was something in the bog that he would find extremely amusing.

A minute later he came out with a white face, sat down, shivered a little, and said, 'I think that was in extremely bad taste.'

I said, 'What do you mean, didn't you see it?'

Through gritted teeth he hissed, 'You know what I mean.'

I said, 'What *do* you mean – the *soap*?'

He said, 'You know,' as he pushed his tuna fish salad out of nostril range. I didn't know why my description of the soap should have distressed him so much and went back into the lavatory and saw a pair of legs sticking out under one of the doors. Knowing that no-one could be that tall, I opened the door of the cubicle to find a man about twenty-eight years old with his trousers round his knees, shirt up to his armpits, lying flat on the floor with a small pool of blood under his head. I realized what Tim meant by bad taste and went to find the Bormann-like manageress. We carried the unfortunate toiletee outside and laid him on the pavement. I made sure that his heart was still beating and that his airway was clear, and examined him for signs of drug overdosage. We found out later that he'd taken LSD and run over and killed an old man with his truck and that his behaviour that evening was his equivalent of joining the Foreign Legion.

1. Quite a nice girl really. I only wrote 'tart' because the back of my neck is aching and I keep being interrupted by telephone calls from Eire about whether *The Life of Brian* is blasphemous, while being interviewed by the Belgians on the same subject.

I had never been to Spain before and was about to start now. Even the foreignness of the place seemed alien, except for my pipe, several packets of 'Three Nuns' and 'St. Bruno' mixed and the odd gin and slimline tonic with ice but no lemon in it. We arrived at the villa which was the upper apartment of a two-floor building, very spacious with two balconies and absolutely covered in fucking bougainvillea, so picturesque it made you want to excrete.

The next day I hired a bicycle and so did John Cleese. He couldn't ride his, but then he was only twenty-five years old. I was worried about the aesthetics of people of that age who are quite capable of basking in the sun wearing only a jock-strap, and of leaving the door open when they go poohs. I realized later that he had gone to a public school, where it's obligatory to be peered at in your most intimate moments (unless you're bullying someone).

John and I had written a lot of sketches for David Frost, as you should know by now if you've been paying attention. In consideration for our services Mr Frost wisely chose to pay us the kind of pittance that we would think a fortune to write a film. David P. Frost had had a very good idea for a motion picture, probably bought from some impecunious city stock-broker. It was a good idea about someone who used psephol-ogy to become first of all Prime Minister and then President of Great Britain. People read in the newspapers about the way they thought and which way they would vote and this influenced them into voting the way the psephologist wanted. The film predicted the advent of the Heath govern-ment, North Sea Gold, twenty-three assassinations, the entire demise of the Anglican Church, and the use of refer-enda by weak governments as a devious means of strength-ening their arm – the public were at first impressed at their new-found power (being asked about such important issues as the Common Market, Trade Unions and Devolution), later becoming pissed off with letter-boxes full of forms ask-ing them about road-widening in the Scilly Isles, the colour of pillar-boxes, and the repeal of the Dog Licensing Act (1878), pissed off to such an extent that after a month they were begging for a dictatorship. In this way a little-known psephologist became the first President of Great Britain.

But Columbia-Warner-Seven Arts decided not to put the film on general release until all the predictions had come true, losing a lot of money for themselves and giving John Cleese, Graham Chapman and Peter Cook nothing for two years' work. If the head of Columbia-Warner-Seven Arts is reading this book he had better be warned that I might at this very moment be outside his door with an ice-axe. I think I can say with sincerity that I'm against any large organization, communist, capitalist or religious, that pretends to know best. I would rather have a perverted Roman Emperor or a pederast king than the blinkered and bureaucratic pismires who trammel humanity with their legal systems, medicine, trade unions, armies, the archaic tribal mutilation of circumcision, baton charges against students, students charging police, fish fingers, lard, turgid or tit-and-bum journalism, television programmes that wouldn't appeal to a stuffed walnut, and National Parades.

Personal masturbation is a noble pastime – enhancing as it does the faculty of imagination – but, as acted out on a national scale becomes true to its Victorian name of self-abuse. Viz. the Trooping of the Colour, Bastille Day, May-day in Moscow, July 4th in America, Timepiece Afternoon in Switzerland, Football matches in Brazil, and anything at all that happens in Germany or Japan. I mean, let's all of us come off it. What are we? We are tubes – hollow cylinders of flesh. What is our expectation from life? Regular fulfilment of primitive functions at both ends, coupled with the thought that we must progress, leaving at least something behind us, very much in the same way that a dog pisses on a tree.

By now all of you must be wondering why we needed to hire bicycles in order to write. I'll explain. As John pointed out, transport on Ibiza at that time was rather primitive and we needed individual conveyances so that we could examine beaches[1] in the shortest time – say about two weeks of the working period which was three months anyway, and 'there's plenty of time yet'. 'I think we should have bikes, because we're bound to want to go off and buy pens and pieces of paper, and pens and things, and Scotch tape, and a pair of

1. To find out which would be the best one for writing a film set in London.

scissors . . . typewriter ribbons . . . well, it took me two weeks to get acclimatized . . . and I still haven't thrown off this throat. . . .'

John Cleese, whom I'd always known as an over-industrious, painstakingly meticulous worker, appeared to be hinting at something.

'It is rather hot isn't it? I'm feeling a bit groggy myself. Perhaps a couple of weeks' rest might be a good idea.'

'D'you think we should? I mean David and all that . . . He has paid us, Graham.'

'Yes, I suppose you're right.'

'Yeah . . . I'll probably be all right tomorrow morning . . . Right . . . yes . . . that's fine then. . . .'

'Fine.'

'Great. . . . Oh shit, d'you mind if we make it evening? Only I promised I'd take Connie to Calla Bassa tomorrow – she's only got a few more days here and it'd be a bit awkward to get out of now. . . . Damn.'

'Oh that's fine by me. I've only just finished taking those bloody exams. We have done the synopsis and I wouldn't mind taking a bit of time off.'

'So we'll start on Friday.'

'Yup. . . . It'll be a bit noisy, but we can shut ourselves away.'

'Noisy?'

'Yes – there's a fiesta, lots of dancing and fireworks, and wine.'

'Oh. I've never been to Spain before.'

'Haven't you? Well you must then. . . . So let's have a look at the diary. That brings us to Monday. We'll start on Monday. Oh, but Monday and Tuesday are Connie's last two days, I'd like to see her off at the airport on Wednesday. That would give us two days . . .'

'Look, why don't we make it two weeks?'

'Done.'

So we closed up our notebook marked 'Film' and went to the beach.

Something had changed in John. Perhaps it was the atmosphere of the island – the singing heat, the occasional fennel-scented breeze castrating the almost ever-present frenzy of the shrill cicadas as we passed through groves of olive and sweet-scented asphodel, looked down into coves of limpid deepest blue that seemed perilously inviting from our vantage point, while in the air was the pitiful bray of a distant donkey being done in by dagos, and the even more distant hum of telephone wires as travel agents desperately tried to contact Lawrence or Gerald Durrell for their latest offer of twenty-five redolent adjectives for 15p in a plain wrapper.

As we cycled adverbially through the adjectival groves of whatever they were – kind of tree-things – in a detached way I looked at the three of us. There was Connie – Constance Booth, later to become John's wife (and ex-wife), who wasn't there that day anyway because she'd gone by boat. There was John, the pedestrian parentally predestined solicitor, changed to a cycle-riding, lobster-red, writer-performer, wearing baggy shorts, plimmies, *no* shirt, sunglasses with white plastic nose-shield, and a floppy khaki hat. ('Crumbs! What a change,' I thought, as we swerved to avoid a dying donkey.) But then this island was already beginning to have its influence on me as well. My first day I had gone down to the beach wearing brogue sandals, tweed swimming shorts, a pair of bakelite Dr Scholl sunglasses, and a straw deerstalker, and now here I was wearing just a pair of denim shorts. What was happening to me? The thought of this blattering transformation made my left hand sweat as it gripped a copy of *The Daily Telegraph*[1] to the handlebars.

There was a loud roar from behind us padded out with ear-shattering horn-blasts. We skidded to a halt at the side of the road to avoid the monstrous vehicle. A SEAT 600 glid past and screeched to a halt in a flurry of sand and donkey-clippings. Marty Feldman's head popped up through the sun-roof like Marty Feldman's head through a sun-roof. As the famous scriptwriter of the radio comedy *Round the Horne*, he was so anxious not to be recognized that he'd been forced to wear no shoes, purple bikini briefs, a half-length orange caftan with purple embroidery, a necklace of golden prayer-bells, and a yellow skullcap with a subtle application of Helena Rubenstein 'Nasolube' nose highlighter. He shouted, 'Did you see the accident?'

1. Which I only took for the crossword (see note on page 55).

'D'you mean this?' said John, pulling his bicycle out of a bush.

'No.'

'The donkey?' I opined,[1] thinking that it must be at least 25,062 words since anyone had done so.

'No – that geezer being pulled out of the well. Tell you at the beach bar.'

'Vroom,' went his SEAT 600.

For the next week we all had Fun going to the beach during the day, trying to find more expensive restaurants in the evening, and having witty and zany conversations. A typical beach scene would be John's Doctor Scholl sunglasses with nose-shield reading *The Daily Telegraph* from cover to cover – they were apparently desperate to learn about politics, football and cricket; Tim Brooke-Taylor running around a lot in the sand; Loretta covered in Sellotape in a desperate attempt to get the gullies in her crow's-feet as brown as the rest of her face, drinking gallons of Buck's Fizz; and Marty amusing the others and himself by annoying John. He spent some time searching out what he thought was the most boring person on the beach and found him. A greengrocer from Nottingham. He was a man of about five foot nine inches, wearing a beach shirt and matching shorts covered with the words SKOL, CHEERS, SALUD, UP YOURS MATE!, SANTÉ, PROUST, EIE HTEIA and a rather inexplicable DAMON RUNYON just under his left tit. Presumably even the shirt printer had found him boring.

Marty told him that he had a friend on the beach who had a copy of yesterday's *Daily Telegraph* (therefore the latest cricket-scores and information about the World Cup) and was also passionately interested in bullfighting, although he'd never seen one. He homed in on John like a missile programmed to injure Frank Sinatra. He warmed up with detailed enquiries about the Third Test, followed by a cripplingly fine-toothed analysis of the England line-up for the World Cup. John very politely answered all his questions, but it was obvious from the pucening of the bald patch at the back of his head that he was growing irritated with the wholesale fruiterer and his greengroçulent attentions.

1. See Chapter 2, page 46.

Yesterday's Daily Telegraph

'Have you ever been to a bullfight?' asked the man.

'No,' John screamed, and ran off towards the sea explaining that he'd promised his auntie that he would bathe regularly, and please, please, keep the *Daily Telegraph*, and that he probably wouldn't be back tomorrow.

'Good idea! Feel like a dip,' said the man and dashed off after him.

John swam what must have been a quarter of a mile underwater without coming up for breath, only to surface next to the Nottinghamshire fruiterer. None of us could hear what was said but the stout Midlander appeared to be demonstrating bullfighting techniques from his lilo. John swam out to sea and was never seen again. (Except a bit.)

I spent the next two weeks on a Cleeseless Ibiza, searching for something that I knew was probably very sexy. I had telephoned my girl friend and she 'Very likely wasn't going to come out', which was a bit of a relief in that I'd rather half-heartedly decided to marry her. A telegram arrived at the villa for 'Dr G. Chapman' and I realized that I'd passed the exams.

Unfortunately so did everyone else on Ibiza. Even the locals didn't trust the two doctors on the island: the 'physician' in S. Antonio, who would dress minor wounds while smoking and patting a scrofulous black labrador; and a surgeon in Ibiza town who refused to attend any emergencies while he was eating breakfast, elevenses, lunch, afternoon tea, dinner or supper. But the human body has remarkable recuperative powers, and, as far as I know only four people died through lack of Aesculapian attention, while in the same period at least eight were killed by nuns posing as medical auxiliaries. The chemists did the rest of the work. The peasants could buy toothpaste with penicillin in it – guaranteed to give them a raging fungal gingivitis – they were given barbiturates for headaches, and quail-flavoured suppositories for everything else. Contraceptives were readily available to kings and popes who rolled their own at 350 Newfoundland kopecks per pair.

Because of this I got several patients (silly complaints) and while dressing the kneecap of Pippa Sherman I realized that I was a doctor and should perhaps consult myself about a psychological complaint. Why was I looking wistfully at the stars every night? Why did I go to so many bars? Why did I avoid the company of the others and yet go out looking for company? Why was I coveting my neighbour's ox?

It was the Quatorze juillet, and having had at least catorce Cuba Libras, I sat smoking my pipe at an outside bar, wondering if I'd see the ox. The coveted animal passed, a nineteen-year-old beauty, small and slim but strongly built, with legs like a Russian ballet-dancer, smooth brown skin, huge dark brown eyes, provocative lips, a retroussé nose, and earlobes that defy description.

He glanced in my direction. He glanced in everyone's direction. I thought, 'Fucking hell, he's a goer if ever I saw one,' which I hadn't (male that is). I nonchalantly threw my *Daily Telegraph* to the floor and with a pounding heart followed at a discreet distance. He was walking towards the campsite in S. Antonio and, leaving all thoughts of the *Daily Telegraph* and my bicycle behind, I tried to look as though I wasn't actually catching up on him. The knowing little flirt stopped on a bridge over a tiny stream. This was it, my catechol amines had reached their lifetime zenith. . . .

Click. Went a tape recorder playback button and David said:

'It was the 14th July, and the campsite was full of French drunks going out as I returned. I liked rising and sleeping early for the sun rather than discos full of Birmingham typists. I was walking on the long road back to the campsite lined with poplars and festive laps dotted with geckos keeping warm.[1] I was saying 'Goodnight' to everyone in any language that seemed to suit their appearance and when I came to saying it in English I think I was answered with 'Good evening' in English from Graham. I thought at first he was coming towards me from the campsite, but it turned out he'd been following me for quite a distance. He asked me what I was doing, and would I like to have a drink at the bar. He told me a strange concocted story about staying one night in the campsite before his room in a villa was ready. He said he'd seen me in town and trailed me a bit.

1. I'm a much more mature writer now (L. Durrell).

'We went to the bar by the swimming-pool. He introduced himself, his work, and ordered two enormous double Bacardi and cokes. We were very amused – making for instant rapport, by the antics of French people dressed in banana-leaves pushing each other into the pool, pouring wine over each other's heads and bellowing every national anthem they knew.

'After quite a few drinks. . . .'

Click. 'Well. We had a polite conversation about the other occupants of the villa who included, intriguingly, Marty Feldman of *Round the Horne*, and his wife – more interesting to me than Cleese or Chapman. . . . Then suddenly Graham asked if he could come and see my tent, which seemed eccentric from such a straight and ordinary-looking man. I genuinely had no inkling until we got there and he was supposedly surveying it that he was actually going to grab me and give me a passionate kiss. That led to seeing the inside of the tent. I was totally amazed at the novelty of it to him. We didn't do anything devastating but spent the time exploring each other – great fun – not heavy and have your rocks off immediately. It was romantic. Still, it was a year before I could believe I wasn't being taken for a ride.

'The night was also punctuated by drunk Frenchmen tripping over guy-ropes regularly till the early hours. Both of us shared a dislike for French people *en masse*, who are almost worse than Germans, although the English are probably worst of all. Still, French women with pinnies, curlers, budgies, tortoises, etc. are as bad as the Americans.

'Graham left the tent at about six in the morning to be chased by the camp alsatian, and was questioned at toothpoint by the commandant. But somehow – by being a bewildered Englishman – he talked his way out.

'He was Adonis-like, with a very short Roman hairstyle bleached almost ash-blond, very fit and in fine condition from rugby and rock-climbing, with a week or two's tan, eyes very blue, and smoking a pipe which I thought was impossible for a gay.

'After that we made tentative arrangements to meet again which I didn't believe. The arrangement was he would leave his bike outside the Rosa Negra boutique and it would have a copy of the *Daily Telegraph* stuffed in the back under the saddle. He used to cycle eleven miles into the town to meet me and I think the villa people were intrigued to know what he was doing. . . .'

Click click rattle rattle slam.

'Hello Towser. Towser wowser who's a good boy tickle tickle under the rear armpits. Urrummmmm. Hellooo! David! Hellooo, David! Are you upstairs?'

(*Silence.*)

'DAVID! Where are you?'

'Don't make so much fucking noise, we're in here.'

F.X.: *Door opening.*

GRAHAM: Oh sorry, I didn't know you were recording.

'Yes we are, about you, so get out.'

'Well actually, David, I think we've probably done enough for the moment.'

'Oh great. Fine. I hope it's all right.'

'It sounded very good.'

'Thanks, Dave. God I'm dying for a gin and tonic. That voice-over went on for hours and hours. The same old thing. They were expecting me to make something funny which wasn't. Still, it's a hundred and fifty quid for half a day's work and it'll never be heard anyway.'

(GRAHAM *sits. Slurp, slurp, slurp and slurp.*)

'Did he talk about Ibiza?'

'Yes, I've got quite a bit of that.'

(*Slurp slurp guzzle guzzle.*)

'Did he tell you about the red snapper in the swimming-trunks?'

'Yes.'

'Me hiring the band to embarrass a table full of French tits in a restaurant?'

'Yes.'

'The mad cowboy who used to shoot up the town with his toy pistols?'

'Yes, that was really funny – what a character.'

'I think I need another of these. Fancy one?'

(ALEX *shakes his head.*)

(*Glug glug. Schweppesss! Glug glug glug. Slurp.*)

Ah that's better . . . I remember J. B. Priestley once gave me his description of the English character. It was at his house near Stratford-on-Avon. Barry Cryer and I, one Friday morning, were hurriedly trying to finish a script for Ronnie Corbett's situation comedy series *No That's Me Over Here*, and the bar was about to open. We wrote 'End of Part One' which completed the first half, and we thought, 'We'll easily finish the rest this afternoon.' We rushed off to the bar dutifully – we took it as a slight if we weren't the first script-writers in. We only just managed to beat Bernard McKenna who at that time was writing some blurb for the *TV Times*.

We all downed a few pints of lager before even the Sports Department had entered – a very cheery lot of non-professional drinkers, who pretend to be butch by punching each other in the balls and telling filthy jokes that everyone's heard before. If there's one thing I can't stand, it is being told jokes. Bernard and I had an intra-company feud with the Sports Department. We would send them messages through the internal mail containing banana peel, bits of dried apricot, cigarette ash, etc., and rearrange their offices for them in the hope that we would hear a wrestling commentary over a horse-race. I'd decided this was High Noon. The showdown of Comedy *vs* Sports was on.

Being wheeled around by Barry on a beer-barrel trolley after having announced that all the Sports Department were pansies, wearing a Gay Lib badge, I attempted to kiss each of them. They resisted fiercely (except for Jimmy Hill, who really is a 'good chap') and stopped punching each other in the balls. I then asked to be wheeled over to a table where I thought I detected two extremely uptight gentlemen who were wearing uptight clothes and talking very earnestly about uptight business. By now I was sitting on the trolley, glid beside them, and said, 'Hello, I'm homosexual.' They looked uneasy until I explained to them I wasn't going to rape them on the spot, and that I'd been living with a steady boyfriend for some years, and could be a useful member of society. They seemed to understand, even bought me a drink, and we finished up talking about sex as though it were something natural. I waved goodbye to the Head of Religious

Broadcasting and his friend and joined a very cheerful Barry in another corner of the bar.

Barry, Bernard, and Richard O'Sullivan (who was doing amazing tricks with cigarettes), sat there for a while, realizing that we'd trounced the Sports Department and thinking about who should be the next victim. After a few lagers we all decided childishly to pick on an innocent but effete (which is also nearly effeminate) director of Light Entertainment who had just appeared in the bar. He stood, trying not to look effete or effeminate, talking to a group of important-looking people who were obviously to do with the production of some terrible trashy programme he was trying to get off the ground. He was some distance from us, but we decided that we would laugh every time he opened his mouth. The rest of the bar couldn't understand our laughter and thought we were just pissing around as usual. But as the director carried on opening his mouth, we began to laugh in earnest to the extent that Bernard McKenna, after twenty minutes of it, was actually able to wring out his handkerchief.

After a tough lunchtime like this, Barry and I trudged back to our office to complete the script. Now for years Barry Cryer had been eulogizing J. B. Priestley – a very good man I thought, but no need to go on about him to the point of nausea. I said, 'Let's go and see him.' Barry said, 'What?' and cavalagerially I said, 'Why not? Let's give him a ring. I'm doing a show in Coventry next week, which is quite close to his house, you're coming to the show, ring him up and we'll pop round to see him for tea.'

Barry almost as cavalagerially, rang up to find the great J.B.'s number from his agent's office, and then dialled the Priestley household.

'Hullow,' said J.B.

'Hullow,' said Barry, after climbing back onto his chair.

Barry explained that there were three TV scriptwriters who'd like to come and have a chat with him, that they would be in his area, and loved his work so much. He said, 'It's not an interview is it?' Barry said, 'No,' and he said, 'See you on Monday afternoon at four.'

Barry was so overwhelmed he stapled his nostrils together. Next Monday we arrived at the house at the appropriate time

– a very pauntly house I may add – and pulled the bell chain. As no-one arrived for some time, John Cleese, G. Chapman and David Sherlock, who were by now accompanying Barry Cryer on his pilgrimage, stood waiting. Barry jokingly did obeisance on his knees to the very front door of his hero, which was unfortunately observed by the maid as she opened the door. We were shown through the marbled corridor to His study, admired the flamingoes in the pond, stared at ninety-five million books written by J. B. Priestley, sat down, and were all suitably ill at ease, with the exception of the lager-and-by-now-gin-and-slimline-tonic-with-ice-but-no-lemon-in-it-sodden me. A thing called polite conversation was made, which bored me rigid. Why should anyone be so much in awe? J.B., being the extremely intelligent man that he is, sensed this, and started to talk about the only subject that he had in common with any of us, which turned out to be my pipe, a quite respectable Dunhill. We chatted about the different sizes and shapes, and the fact that Ralph Richardson sends him a Dunhill every year because of a successful run he'd done in a Priestley play, *An Inspector Calls*, I think it's called, although I'm not very attentive.

After a few garbled and inept nothings from us (with the exception of pipes) we went through to the lounge to have tea and cucumber sandwiches with his wife, Jacquetta Hawkes. I think all of us felt that we could ask the question, 'Now please tell me everything about the world,' and that he and she could have given a reasonable answer. While talking about some work that had been done, but done incorrectly, in the garden, he made a remark I liked about English people. He explained that the biggest fault of the English, but perhaps their most charming attribute, was that they had one foot in America, and the other in Mexico.

We tittered grovellingly. I had another cucumber sandwich and said to Jacquetta, 'These are delicious, but are you any good at doing links?'

'Of course I am,' she said. 'I'm doing one now.' And so, from cucumber sandwiches we turn to Essene manuscripts. And from that immediately to Ibiza, on July 20th 1966.

Thanks, Big J., that was really super.

The weather had been ideal for six weeks and encouraging naughty behaviour in twenty-five-year-old adolescents.

I'd been meeting David furtively on lonely beaches, with the inhabitants of the villa, particularly Loretta Feldman, wondering where I was spending my time. I didn't want anyone to know of my shameful behaviour, but the idea of a portion of naughtiness in a real bed overwhelmed me. Which is why, very grown-up and hairy though I was, I woke up one morning to find myself in bed with a young gentleman.

Someone was trying to get into my room which, with the precaution of a drunk, I had locked the night before. Knock! knock! knock! went the door. I froze as though it was Armageddon. Knock! knock! knock! went the bloody door again.

'Hello Graham,' said Humphrey Barclay from outside. He had never offered me coffee before and I think had sussed out that something naughty had been going on in my room. I shouted, 'NO, THANK YOU!' in capitals and added, 'I'll see you soon,' while turning vermilion.

I signalled David into silence, unlocked the door and walked out with all the nonchalance of a guilty child-molester. I went into the kitchen and saw H.B. Why was he still there? He should have been on the beach. I looked out of the window and saw the clouds. It was the one dull day. Julian Slade had decided to stay at home and paint on the verandah. Alan Hutchieson was doing sketches in the main bedroom. Marty and Loretta Feldman were not quite having it off but with the door open. And so I stood in the kitchen making small talk with H. such as, 'Oh dear, it's a dull day, perhaps it will rain.'

'Yes it does look dull,' said Humphrey. 'It might even rain. Why was your door locked? . . . You've got a scratch on your back.'

'Oh it's nothing, must have hit a wall or something.'

'Whose are those pears?'

'Tim's I think.'

While he was sorting out the salt for his egg, I surreptitiously stuffed a pear down the front of my trunks and while saying, 'Ugh! it was a late night. See you later,' I went into the corridor outside my bedroom and threw the pear onto the bed containing David, in a kind of pathetic breakfastorial gesture. I quickly whispered an arrangement to meet him that evening in the bar near the Rosa Negra. At the same time I explained to him the need to be v.v. silent and that I would move down the corridor, wait until H. Barclay was engaged in the kitchen and Alan Hutchieson wrapped up in roughing the outline of a tree and Julian Slade was more fully engrossed in the tinting of his fucking bougainvillea.

It was arranged that I should sit on the sofa in the main room until such time as the desired situation had been met. From the sofa I could see all three people doing their things. I coughed once while they were all looking at their own activities, which gave David time to dash out of my bedroom into the corridor. Looking around with affected ease I waited for another convenient moment and coughed again, this time incredibly loud, so that everyone would look at me rather than David who was rushing down the stairs and out.

'He looks nice,' said Julian as he looked down from his painting, not realizing who'd just walked past. 'Who's that Jules?' said Humphrey, rushing onto the balcony.

'I don't know, never seen him before. Very brown isn't he? What a tan! And I bet that's all over. . . .'

'Have you seen him before Graham?' asked Humphrey.

'Good grief, no . . . probably just walking past.'

'You mean the one eating the pear?' asked Julian.

'No that huge bloke,' said Humphrey, 'the one all covered in grease, sand, and donkey fluff.' 'Where, where?' asked Julian.

'The one wearing the athletic support and the Manchester United bathing cap. . . . It's . . . it's . . . it's John! He's back!'

John Cleese (for it was he) took a bionic leap and arrived on the roof of the house next door, unconscious. We dragged him down and revived him with caffeine enemas, but he was soon in good shape, and, wrapped in a blanket, he sat on the sofa and told us, as we all listened with characteristically bated breath, his ridiculous yarn about how he'd just swum from Wembley, having seen England beat West Germany in the final of the World Cup.

Marty Feldman and Loretta arrived, dressed with their usual modesty as D'Artagnan and Kemal Ataturk. They wondered where John had been, where I had been, and what the score had been. '4–2,' said John. 'That greengrocer isn't around still is he?'

'No,' said Marty.

'Who was that throwing pears away?' asked Loretta.

'No idea,' I said.

'He had gorgeous eyes.'

'We've just got some tickets for a bullfight tonight. We can all go,' said Marty. All except me cried, 'Great, great.'

'Oh damn! We only got seven.'

'Don't worry, John can have mine,' I said. 'I thought I'd just wander around town a little, I want an early night anyway and the throat's still playing up.'

They seemed not to notice anything wrong with my excuse, and I left soon after for town with a song in my thighs.

I threw my bicycle and *Daily Telegraph* down in the dust under a tree near the Rosa Negra, and ran upstairs to the balcony bar. I was nervous, and swallowed two swift Cuba Libras, and went to look for David. He was there, sitting at a table on the edge of the balcony. We spent half an hour exchanging rather wet conversation, with me pretending to be interested in theatre and him pretending to be interested in television. Then

I heard John talking to Connie outside the boutique below us. The whole party had returned early from the bullfight, having found the sight of an inept killer of bulls repellent. John didn't feel like a drink, neither did Connie, so they both went off. Marty, Loretta and the rest were off not being noticed somewhere, but Alan Hutchieson said, 'See you later, I think I'll just have a quick one and a look at the crossword.'

I heard him climbing the stairs and, with fear threatening the hygiene of my underpants, I told David I'd see him later at the floating bar in the harbour, and fled to the bog. I was in a hell of a state. David was deliberately wearing tightly suggestive clothes and I couldn't be seen with him – certainly not by a reporter from *The Times*. Through the keyhole I could see Alan, who sat down opposite David and read almost every word in *The Times* before starting on the crossword.

After about an hour the waiters were beginning to make even louder knocking noises on the door – there was only one bog.

Half an hour later the constant pounding reminded me of sitting in a public convenience in Dresden on St. Valentine's Day 1945. I made being ill noises, simulating vomiting and worse, and even considered jumping out of the window into the street below, but then Alan was facing in that direction and would have seen me anyway. He wouldn't move. Why not? He ordered another drink and went back to the crossword – I nearly went mad. Another bang on the door. I made more vomiting noises in Spanish.

Finally he asked for the bill, and haggled agonizingly over the tip. I was hoping David hadn't left our rendezvous, as I was still uncertain of his affection for me, and I knew he had some French git as a 'friend' on the island. As soon as I saw Alan leave and get on his bike, I unlocked the door and came out rubbing my stomach and going 'Eurrgh!' in front of irate dago waiters.

I ran down the streets to the harbour and into the bar. David was there. Because I imagined my 'offence' to be punishable by shame and social rejection in perpetuity (and being kneed in the groin by the police whenever they had a moment to spare), there was nowhere for us to go except beside some uncomfortable rocks just beyond the harbour. But lying down under the stars with the person I loved, I couldn't think that any bug-eyed monster from another world would have objected. And even God has his compassionate moments, presumably.

The next morning we were all having coffee (a euphemism for gin and slimline tonic with ice but no lemon in it, in my case) and just as I was making excuses for not going to the same beach as the others, we saw what appeared to be, and was, David Paradine Frost walking up the street. He had just arrived, having popped over from London for lunch to see how John and I were getting on with the script. He'd no idea where we were staying but then Ibiza is a small island for a man who thinks he's that big. We called out to him. He joined us and chatted intermittently about the film and how super everything was, while signing autographs for English tourists.

He ended up staying one-and-a-half-days – a record holiday. Tim and I took him out to eat and using one of the least sophisticated drugs in the world – alcohol – saw through the outer shell of his psyche to find surprisingly pleasant contents. The sort of man, rather like John Cleese, with whom you would feel you had more in common, if only they drank as much as you did.

Several years later I went to see David at his home in London on a purely friendly visit. He couldn't understand this and was certain that I was trying to sell him something, like a television or film script. I wasn't, but even after reading this I'm sure he'll suspect that I still am.

On his last morning in Ibiza David (F) wanted to go to the beach. The others had all left by then – or hadn't come back – how the hell am I supposed to remember everything – I mean it's difficult writing autobiographies you know – specially when you're doing it with someone else. I'd arranged to meet David (S) at Calla Bassa, but since there was no-one else in the house to look after David (F) I couldn't leave him alone. I said, 'Let's go to Calla Bassa, it's a nice beach,' half hoping that David (S) wouldn't show up, since I'd got my boss with me. The two of us rode down to S. Antonio, but unfortunately the last boat had left for Calla Bassa.

David (F) has never even had a daunt: and wasn't about to then. Without speaking a word of Spanish, he shoved 59,000 pesetas into the hands of a previously lazing dago, and off we went, just the two of us on a caique that would normally carry seventy people.

At Calla Bassa David romped around the beach attempting to play football – I didn't want to join in – and amused himself paddling in three feet of water. He can't swim. He was wearing my snorkel and goggles and became more and more amused and high-pitched in his description of the tiny animals called fish that he'd previously only ever seen in restaurants. In the water, without his girdle, in profile he resembled Alfred Hitchcock. But it was good to see him enjoying himself outside a board meeting. He joined me at the beach-bar and so did David (S). And like St Peter I pretended he was only a casual acquaintance.

And on the way back to the airport David (F) said, 'That boy on the beach?'

'Oh yes,' I said, still hoping to avoid the issue.

'You know, the one with the big eyes that came up and spoke to us. He's a nice young man. He's a homosexual isn't he?'

I said, 'Probably,' and he said, 'It's a pity isn't it?'

I didn't say it but inside I thought, 'Damn you – no it fucking isn't.'

CHAPTER SEVEN

A Reincarnation

In the course of David Frost's 'One-day Holiday' in Ibiza he checked up that John and I had actually been doing some writing and even 'squawked' at it, which we took for laughter (but he pointedly looked forward to reading more than ten pages); said that he thought that it'd be a good idea if John Cleese, Tim Brooke-Taylor, Marty Feldman and myself did a TV comedy show together; and added that he was looking for something for Ronnie Corbett to do, remarking 'Perhaps you, Graham and Barry Cryer would like to have a go at writing it – a kind of middle-class situation comedy – there hasn't really been one.'

That all sounded very good to me. Although I knew him, I'd never written with Barry[1] before. 'How would it be if Eric Idle, Barry and myself were to write a pilot programme for the series?'

---

1. Whom you, dear reader, should know slightly better now than I did then.

'Super,' said David. 'Super,' and went off to frolic in the shallow waters.

And so what was to become *The Rise and Rise of Michael Rimmer*, later re-written with Peter Cook; *At Last the 1948 Show* (very much a progenitor of *Python*); and several series of Ronnie Corbett's *No That's Me Over There* would never have happened if it hadn't been for forty-five minutes of David Frost's enthusiasm and confidence prior to paddling.

When I returned from Ibiza I had three months to fill in before taking up an Ear, Nose and Throat 'House-job', and a secure future in medicine seemed to be mapped out for me. Too secure, too mapped out. If I carried on in medicine, I realized I'd have a pretty good idea exactly what I'd be doing ten, twenty and even thirty years from that moment. It struck me like a halibut from the North Sea that that was not the way my life should go at all. What was the point of working on through up to the age of sixty-five and then taking a chance on a better reincarnation next time?

Instead of filling in with an E.N.T. locum I decided to see if I could 'earn' money by writing 'professionally' and so I wrote sketches for Roy Hudd – a programme called the *Illustrated Weekly Hudd*, and, for a little extra money at Christmas, wrote the linking material for a Petula Clark show. The sketches for Roy came easily enough; it was like writing for *The Frost Report*. But trying to think up seven different introductions for 'The Other Man's Grass is Always Greener' and ten for 'Downtown' and the odd humorous remark for such people as Sacha Distel, Anthony Newley and Johnny Mathis was really quite a feat. Despite this, I was hooked by it all. It was Showbiz for Dr G. . . .

The pilot script for Ronnie Corbett was approved and the three of us wrote the scripts for seven programmes. Eric, not finding sit-com was his trunk of marbles, opted out leaving Barry and me to go on and write a further forty-seven half-hour programmes. The first of these got very little critical attention. I think the *Sun* newspaper quite liked it. George Melly in the *Observer* hated it. But then, most unusually for a critic, George Melly, after having seen the second programme, recanted completely with an enthusiastic review ending '*Mea culpa!*' 'A friend for life,' I thought. Ronnie

Corbett got pretty good viewing figures too, which rather annoyed John Cleese, as our very own *At Last the 1948 Show* was less widely seen.

But *1948* did get a lot of favourable attention from the Press and quite a cult following and Marty Feldman rocketed overnight to Intergalacticsuperstardom. After his own BBC show won the 'Platinum Hydrangea of Montreux' award he 'zapped-off Stateside-wards-ville' for a wallooming career in the Movies.

Between the first run of seven and the second of six *1948* shows I was living with David in a flat in Hampstead.

The Coming Out Party

22 Gayton Crescent, nineteen sixty-thing.

'Bring-bring', said the telephone.[1]

'It's all right, Dave, I'll get it.'

'Bring-bring' it opined again,[2] and before I could stop him Dave had picked up the handset and was answering. I rushed up and thumped him across the gob to stop him saying any more.

'Who was that?' said my mother.

'Oh it was one of the painters,' I said, knowing that she knew I was decorating my flat.

'It sounded like one of the painters I've spoken to before.'

'Well, yes, it probably did a bit.'

'It's a bit late for a painter isn't it?'

'No. No, you just don't understand London, mother. This is not like Leicester.' For a whole year I had lived in terror, an almost thorpeian terror, of being found out for what I was – a

1. A slight inaccuracy (see page 109). It was more like 'Bleunngg-bleunngg'.
2. See 1.

Fuck it, I thought. Why go through this agony? I decided that I would invite all my closest friends to a party to meet David and explain to them all that I was a bit 'bent'. The agony of keeping silent had become too great. Having to explain to Marty, John and Tim that I had to 'rush off to St Swithin's to cash a cheque', when I should have been writing with them at 10 o'clock in the evening, became boring, worrying and unnecessary. I thought, why hide something from intelligent people like that. I was ashamed that I wasn't admitting that Dave was my closest friend. He came to most of the recordings of *The 1948 Show* and sat at the back anonymously in the audience and couldn't come with all the other people's wives and girlfriends to the bar after the recordings. I felt unable, stupidly, to take David there. I always noticed him in the audience and we exchanged a glance or two but I even felt ashamed of doing that.

So, after a year, I decided that this party would be a good idea to get it all out into the open once and for all. I invited Marty, John, Tim, Eric Idle, Barry Cryer, Dick Vosburgh and Beryl – almost everyone that I knew – I don't think David Frost could make it, he was in a meeting at the time – and even my ex-girlfriend, and one or two other people from St Swithin's. This was a 'Coming-out Party'.

We laid on a very good meal in our little basement flat, a buffet. We had splendid food and lots to drink, because I still felt a bit nervous about the occasion, and I thought I'd better get everyone pretty pissed before making – well, not an announcement – just wandering from group to group explaining that this was David and introducing him. And that's what I did. It was interesting seeing various people's reactions to this. From Marty, it wasn't so much surprise, as disbelief, but then laughter – being an East-End lad brought up in a theatrical family with a telluric wife he wasn't worried about it at all. And obviously he had met similar people before – he was a B.A. (first class honours with distinction) from the University of Life (Commercial Road College). He was telluric too, it was fine, and I felt a little bit relieved about that. I then went on to chat to the others.

John Cleese already knew about it because I thought that just to announce it to him, since he was one of my closest friends and we wrote together, would be tactless or even a form of betrayal. I'd actually told him about two nights before this party, so he wasn't surprised, but was still in a state of shock about it all, because it was totally, totally alien to him – such a thing was unthinkable and this was going to be the ruin of my life. Although he was still friendly he was completely at a loss to give his feelings. But his girl friend at the time, Pippa, was a lot more understanding. I've often found that women are a lot more understanding about male homosexuality than men; because I suppose men feel threatened in some way. I don't know what it is, but your average butch male is probably worried about certain tendencies and things that went on at school, and now is so bleedin' butch and grimly heterosexual that he wouldn't admit to such a thing even existing, except with scorn or in various puny jokes about people wearing pink and mincing around.

The other reactions: Barry Cryer was fine, he took it all in his stride because of his previous showbiz background – he did write for Danny La Rue, after all. My ex-girlfriend, unfortunately, ran off in tears, accompanied by a couple of people from St Swithin's, so that was a bit of an unhappy moment, but she came to terms with it eventually. The other extraordinary reaction was from Eric Idle, who was quite stunned – obviously he was quite young then, but I had to explain to him what it all meant – that I did actually go to bed with people of the same sex and that it was quite fun and we actually loved each other – it wasn't at all naughty. Now, of course, he's probably even more liberated than I am – not in the same way, but in 750 other ways. Being the only child of a mother who looks exactly like Mary Whitehouse can't have helped to give him an open outlook towards other human beings, or could it?

I felt a lot better after the party.

But it was about two years later than that before I could tell my parents, which was a very difficult moment. By then I had a flat in Belsize Park. They'd visited that flat, and by now they'd spoken to David on the phone and they knew that he was living there. I made elaborate attempts to make it look as though there was a separate bedroom for him and had to rush around the house, hiding things the whole time, to make it look as though I was in the master bedroom sleeping in a large size double bed with no-one else and making sure there were no head marks on the pillow next to mine – literally that sort of detail because my mother would have noticed – as they do. Of course the first thing my mother ever did when she came to the house was want to put her coat in my bedroom, and I knew damn well she'd have a quick pry – look through all the cupboards, under the floor boards etc. I usually tried to insist that I put her coat in my bedroom for her, but she'd always try the door, nevertheless, and go in.

Eventually she got so inquisitive that I had to lock the door. She had always been a bit of a Hercule Poirot. I remember her finding a contraceptive in my pocket when I was about fourteen. I only bought the thing to see what it looked like. It was a question of going into a barber's shop in those days and trying to raise enough courage to ask for one – I think they cost two and nine at the time – for three. I was a tall child for fourteen so it didn't look too unnatural to the barber and I did get the 'Was there anything else?' treatment and said 'Yes, there is,' and promptly gave him 3/9 and got the packet. Partly, I suppose, I wanted to find out what they felt like. And then you never know your luck.

Unfortunately Hercule Poirot found one in my pocket and it was the usual, 'What's this?'

'I think maybe a friend must have put it in my pocket for a joke. I've never seen it before.'

The great detective was rather angry and explained that Mrs Wood's husband, over the road, uses those and they've got five children – it hasn't done them any good has it? My reply to that was, 'What if he'd never used *any*? How many would she have then?'

About a year later than the time when I was hiding things, I decided I'd just have to tell them. It was a waste of my time pretending and a waste of their time worrying. So I told my mother that David was my boy friend. I've never seen such rage, tears, stamping of little feet. It took me quite a long time to calm her down – luckily I was fortified on quite a lot of gin and tonic and was determined in my mind that everything was all right. I'd been in at the inception of the Gay Liberation movement in this country and so had a pretty solid idea that what I was doing was not wrong and that to love another human being, of whatever sex, is surely an admirable thing. I wasn't taking any more, and while she was having her little fit, I stood firm and told her to shut up, that it was all pointless, she'd known David for a couple of years and neither of us had done any harm to the other. Still she screamed. Eventually she calmed down and then I said, 'Right, I'm just going to tell Dad.'

That started her up again: 'Oh no, no don't. It'll kill him.'

'No it won't, it won't.'

'Yes it will, it'll kill him, it'll kill him.'

'It won't, of course it won't. Shut up, I'm going to tell him.'

But eventually she persuaded me that it might have some adverse effect on him and she made me promise not to tell him. So they went home, my mother pretending that nothing had happened at all. She spent the next seven nights completely sleepless, until he eventually forced it out of her and said, 'Look, what the hell's the matter with you?' She explained to my father, who took it all in his stride.

I was on the way back from some show I was doing up north and was going to call in and see them at Leicester. I was too late really to call in and get back to London on time so I rang them up from a motorway service station and explained that I couldn't call. At the end of the conversation my father said, 'Oh Graham, your mother's been a bit upset the last week and I know what it's about. Look, don't worry about it, she doesn't understand these things.' I felt fine, that was good. Thereafter David has been like another son to them and they've been absolutely splendid ever since. But it is very difficult for people to break that kind of news to their parents. They should. What's the point in hiding things and telling lies? That's what I hated, and having to cover up something. I had always had to watch myself on the phone and in conversation:

'What are you doing tomorrow?'

'Oh we're going to . . .'

'What do you mean *we*?'

'Well, ha, ha, no, sorry, I meant I.'

I wouldn't encourage anyone to lie[1] but that's one to watch out for – the 'WE': 'Oh we're just sitting at home watching television – er, I'm just sitting at home watching television.'

I had learnt about the Gay Liberation movement through a German friend of mine called Jurgen, who was the son of a German steel manufacturer that provided a lot of arms for the last war – they were second only to the Krupps. I'm digressing for a moment, but he told me that after the war the school children in Germany were regularly shown films by the Americans of the Nazi atrocities: Jurgen at nine years old saw emaciated corpses dumped into communal graves, people strung up by piano wire and other nauseating antics from Auschwitz, Dachau etc. To show such films to German adults was a bit like rubbing a dog's nose in its own dirt: a bad policy. It's better to be kind to the dog – show him how to behave properly and then reward him. But to do such a thing to children was Freud-blenching.

Anyway Jurgen was the first male person I went with, with any kind of love in my heart, since meeting David. We were both twenty-eight or twenty-nine at the time. He was running a restaurant in Ebury Street which David and I went to virtually every other night – and it was Jurgen who first introduced me to the fact that there were Gay Lib meetings going on.

One night in Jurgen's restaurant there was an American lady who was out with a paid escort. She was on her own in London, a rich, middle-aged, blue-rinsed-hair, Daughter of the Revolution type. She was having a great time, it was her last night in town. She obviously wasn't going to get any-where with her rather young escort but she was enjoying herself. She'd been to the theatre, was enjoying London – because London was a fairly swinging place with the Fab Four, Sergeant Pepper, A Whiter Shade of Pale – to name but two – everyone feeling relaxed and everyone richer too. I was just beginning to earn a little bit of money myself and so felt braver than ever. Anyway to go back to the blue-rinsed lady and the escort . . . at the table opposite them was a group of what you could very well call 'queens', who were being rather precious and superior. They were far more sophisti-

1. That's my prerogative: you write your own autobiography.

cated than this rather crude lady on the table opposite them. The kind of comments they made were really rather annoying. I can't recall them exactly, but you could tell from the atmosphere at the table they were doing a lot of sneering and it angered me. So I took a rose from my table and went and gave it to the lady. She was thrilled by this: that someone at another table should come up and give her a rose, simply because she was a nice person; she was absolutely thrilled by it.

The table full of queens laughed, thinking I was sending her up, so I went over to their table and said, icily, 'That is my mother.' They sank into silence. 'Anyone got anything to say about my mother?' They looked rather embarrassed and ate their meal in silence after that. I just went back to my table and glared frequently at them for the rest of my meal.

I had put some money into *Gay News*, a fortnightly newspaper, to help get it started and my point in doing so was that I thought that it would be valuable if someone, say, in Huddersfield, could buy a paper like that and realize that he wasn't the only homosexual in the world, because in Huddersfield at that time there wouldn't really have been many people that he could have talked to about such things. It would have been difficult for him to talk to a doctor, a priest or a schoolteacher and so he would have had to resort to any outlet he could find, either to pornographic literature, public lavatories, or sitting next to people in cinemas and doing the kneesy-kneesy bit, all of which would have been likely to land him in a great deal of trouble. If someone like him, or indeed her, could find out where to go, like advice centres, clubs or discos – places where there were a lot of people who felt the same way – he or she wouldn't be quite so lonely and there would be fewer suicides. Suicide was quite common amongst lonely gay people in Britain at that time and there was also a thing called police entrapment.[1] There was one incident where a youth (by youth I mean a person under twenty-one years of age), had been with several gentlemen in the district. With promises of leniency the police persuaded him to reveal the names of his lovers. Filled with remorse at what he'd done, he committed suicide: two of the other five

1. Policemen posing as pouffs for proof.

They were doing a lot of sneering

men involved ended their own lives because of the shame of it all. This could not happen today.

Suddenly I feel like digressing for another moment about morality. I intend to publish here for the first time what I believe to be a missing portion of the New Testament. The papyrus manuscript, translated here from the original Greek, was discovered in 1979 by the author at Auckland airport. He was there in transit to Sydney, Australia on the 5th November whiling away a few moments, idly looking under rocks when the manuscript[1] was given to him by a Maori chieftain and toilet attendant.

The First Epistle of Paul the Apostle to the New Zealanders
A.D.59   CHAPTER ONE
1 In which Paul castigateth the Antipodeans; 2, 3, empty showing of holiness; 4 of fornicators and abusers of mankind; 5 of poverty and tolerance; 8 exhorteth them to beware of false prophets.

1. Dear New Zealanders,
    It has come to my attention from our brother Hillary, the Beekeeper of Auckland, that all is not well in your community.
2. What is all this nonsense about certain of your number kneeling down in front of crosses? That is naughty in the extreme; you've changed the glory of an incorruptible God into an image.
3. I understand that the very same people collect together in churches for the purpose of worship. Who needs it? God doesn't. I've asked Him; He's fed up with it, especially psalms, they give Him a headache and cause his teeth to strike together. Don't they realize *their* praise is meaningless? Why can't they concentrate on being better behaved towards one another and forget about this empty show of holiness? He also says, though don't quote me on this, 'They can stuff it up their arses.' He said that, not I. I, a mere mortal, would not have put it quite like that. I'm afraid I think too much about my earthly reputation; but I cannot help agreeing with Him.
4. About fornicators, adulterers, effeminates and abusers of mankind: I am constantly being misquoted on this point. I would like to state quite clearly that sex is nothing more than a way in

1. The manuscript contained two leaves of an Alexandrian text type, similar to the Beatty Biblical Papyrus II P[46]. But this was probably written by a scribe whose native tongue was Coptic. Once the mis-spellings and itacisms are corrected, it closely resembles the Greek of the earlier Alexandrian witnesses.

which two or more people can have lots of harmless cheap fun, provided that they are clean and that the aim is not reproduction. The betterment of the lot of mankind is impossible without strict limits on reproduction, so don't make the mistake the rest of the world has made and over-populate yourselves. Not every-one has to have children, for Christ's sake. He didn't have any, and I should know. If you really feel you have to have chil-dren, then make sure that, as parents, you have no more than you can properly look after. I don't know how all this non-sense about counting souls got started, it just leads to over-crowding and poverty. Look, poverty isn't all it's cracked up to be; I think the old needle / rich man / camel story is being misunderstood out of con-text. Of course worrying about earthly possessions makes it dif-ficult to concentrate on spiritual things but, dear friends, isn't it also difficult to concentrate on spiritual things if you are an ill-nourished, diseased down-and-out. The deprived may also become the depraved.[1]

5. I've had a lot of trouble with this poverty idea in Rome where the notion unfortunately seems to be catching on that the Church should be richer than anyone else on the grounds that only they can handle it. Peter, for instance, scared Ananias and Saphirra to death for hard cash in the name of the Church. I said to him, 'Now, that wasn't very Christ-like, was it?' And he told me to get stuffed as he was a Super-Apostle.

6. You seem to have made more progress in stamping out the primitive tribal mutilation of circumcision than they have in more venal communities, yet it is still recommended, so the Beekeeper tells me, by some wretched 'physicians' who seek to line their pockets or cling to their Judaic ancestry. . . .

7. Talking of tribes, from what I've heard, there could still be more understanding and toler-ance between the two main tribes in your islands. I hope this is heeded more than my letter to the Tasmanians. . . .

8. I exhort you to:
   be empathetic;
   be splendid;
   be aware of your own ignor-ance, and, as always, beware of those who claim to lead you to better self-knowledge by taking your money.

Must finish now as I have to catch the post. Lots of love, P. Kiss, kiss, kiss.

1. See *West Side Story*. You shouldn't sit at home reading books all the time. (G.)

There has been much discussion about the authenticity of this Pauline Epistle. The fact that it predates Captain Cook's voyages is countered by other instances of long distance travel predating Western historical records and carbon 14 and thermoluminescent age verification. Most theologians, however, give little credence to so-called scientific proofs and consider that it could not have been written by Paul in that the writer of this letter finishes his sentences properly, doesn't become over-enthusiastic and get lost when making a point, and also is not rabidly anti-women. However, other biblical scholars point out that the writer's fixation about circumcision and his paranoia about his position as an apostle are typical of St Paul. They believe that this may be one of the few Pauline letters not to have suffered editorially or to have been largely rewritten by second century politico-biblical hacks, since it had been carried swiftly, thousands of miles from the great Bowdlerization-centre in Rome.

CHAPTER EIGHT

Two Films and Six Snakes

After two series of *At Last the 1948 Show*, John Cleese and I decided to spend our time trying to write films and we began work on a film which would have starred Ronnie Barker, Ronnie Corbett, Tim Brooke-Taylor, John Cleese, Graham Chapman and Marty Feldman (in the role of 'Owltruss'). It was only ever provisionally entitled *Renta-sleuth* and was about the misadventures at a security firm who, unknown to themselves, were hired both to protect the secrets of the manufacture of a new nerve gas and at the same time to commit industrial espionage by stealing the plans for its manufacture. We wrote what we considered to be a very funny script and worked on it with the splendid director Charles Crichton, who directed several Ealing Comedies, including *The Lavender Hill Mob*. Unfortunately, we were contractually committed to the Frost Organisation, which meant that the film did eventually get made but was produced by Ned Sherrin under the witty title *Rentadick*. Seeing the way things were going for this venture, John and I refused to take any further part in it.

We did see a screening of the film after which we decided that even our names should be removed from the credits. Otherwise we would have felt like accessories to the theft of our own valuables. I am convinced that the original script could still be filmed: the connection between it and the one Mr Sherrin had produced would be unnoticeable. We fought to have our credits removed. His film does, therefore, have the unique distinction of having the following writers' credits:

[a blank space]
additional material by Jim Viles and Kurt Loggerhead

It was during this period that we were visited by a strange, portly[1] American producer who had heard of 'two new young brilliant English screen-writers'. Having looked him up in the film and TV year-book, we'd come to the decision that his credits amounted to cinematic ordure. John had always had an explicable fondness for soft cuddly toys and stuffed animals, particularly at that stage ferrets and mice. He must have had fourteen or fifteen of them and so before the unpauntly producer arrived in our office we'd arranged for a furry creature to be peering out from behind every picture, out of every cupboard – behind the clock; tails could be seen disappearing under doors and chairs and little pink eyes peered in through the windows. We were anxious to see how he would react. The poor man came in and sat down and began to tell us something of the plot of this marvellous movie. I remember at one point he was saying how we could go anywhere with this picture. He was saying that in one scene we could have the heroes making their exit from a medieval town. We could have 'Ernest Borgnine on a hog and Kirk Douglas on a hog and Jack Palance on a hog, all of them on hogs leaving this town' – couldn't we picture it? We stared at him with growing doubt.

As he tried to continue his story he must have noticed a large number of stuffed animals peering directly at him from various parts of the room. He coughed a couple of times,

1. In no way pauntly.

brought out a handkerchief and thirty or forty brightly coloured tranquillizer pills fell to the carpet. John, the ferrets and I tried not to notice as he picked them up and hurriedly popped a few of them into his mouth and we found ourselves saying that we would let him know. . . .

Imagine our surprise. . . . No, don't, why should you when it's perfectly possible for me to explain it. . . ? A week later John and I were more pleased than we'd ever been to receive a call from Peter Sellers who wondered if we could spare some time – a week, maybe two, to do some re-writing on a film he was about to make called *The Magic Christian*. We said we were interested – we liked the sound of the money particularly and he sent round copies of the original Terry Southern book and screenplay. We found the book rather 'episodic' and too much of its humour relied on the fact that given sufficient money, you can make people do anything, a rather too obvious point. But several of the episodes were extremely funny and we felt we could add to it. One of our main tasks also was to write in a new character to be played by Ringo Starr. Well, we wrote and wrote and wrote and wrote and we wrote quite well, so much so that on the basis of the re-written script the producers were able to raise the money for the project.

Peter Sellers I liked a great deal but he was somewhat insecure in his judgement in that he would fall about having read a scene one evening and we would arrive the next morning to find that this scene 'no longer worked' – Peter's milkman apparently had not laughed at it. While I had a great deal of sympathy for Peter and could understand how difficult it must be for someone in his position really to trust anyone else's judgement, I was angered by the fact that as soon as 'shooting' began, Terry Southern was sent for and the 'original' script reinstated.

I watched the first day's rushes, a scene in which Peter, as Guy Grand, with his purchased son, Youngman Grand (Ringo Starr), was wandering through Sothebys. Peter was handing over enormous quantities of cash for works of art while Ringo followed with a shopping trolley ticking off the list of Rembrandts, Picassos, Modiglianis etc., which, once bought, were thrown carelessly into the trolley, to the distress of the 'Curator' (played by John Cleese) whom they aimed to drive mad. He was torn, as they knew he would be, between his love of fine art and fine money. Finally he had to submit to the indignity of allowing Sir Guy to buy a Rembrandt portrait, the only portion of which Youngman wanted for his collection was the nose (Ringo: 'I only like noses') which his father then promptly cut out, discarding the rest of the painting as so much rubbish.

Ringo got a lot of laughs in the rushes but Peter felt he hadn't really caught his own character quite correctly yet . . . and so the scene was re-shot, but only the end of the scene, cutting out most of Ringo's lines. In his insecurity Peter surrounded himself with more and more friends who would love to take a part, so the final cast was quite phenomenal; such people as Yul Brynner, Wilfred Hyde-White, Lawrence Harvey, Ursula Andress, Spike Milligan, even Roman Polanski. I certainly met a few people from the world of films during the shooting of this picture, but couldn't help feeling that somehow or other everything would have been better if more attention had been paid to the script than to everything being 'Wonderful'. . . . The final result, I suppose, was patchily funny and everyone was extremely good in it, but it was a missed opportunity. . . .

In the spring of nineteen sixty-splunge John Cleese and Graham Chapman thought they might like to do another television programme. In another part of London, Michael Palin, Terry Jones and Eric Idle and an American draft-dodger (and who can blame him?) called Terry (Vance) Gilliam thought they would too. Their last show had been a zany, whacky, dappy, dippy, off-the-wall, over-the-carpet-through-the-french-windows-and-into-the-garden   show which included the splendid Bonzo Dog Doo-Dah Band with His Pauntliness, Neil Innes. . . . This 'effort' was a children's programme called *Do Not Adjust Your Set*.

Barry Took, ex-writing partner of Marty Feldman, conceived the notion that perhaps six of us could produce an intercoursingly-good-show. I was unaware of this at the time, but I have been told that one of the strong reasons for the amalgamation of the two groups was John Cleese's shall we say 'affection'? for 'Mikey' (as he calls him) Palin, but I know nothing of these things . . . and he certainly doesn't.

This then was the beginning of *Owl-Stretching-Time, The Toad-Elevating-Moment, A-Horse-A-Bucket-A-Spoon, Sex-And-Violence, Circus, Flying Circus, Gwen Dibley's Flying Circus,* and eventually *Monty Python's Flying Circus,* and now *Python.*

I remember not being particularly interested in the debate about titles and wouldn't have minded if the programme had been called *Lizard* in that the contents of the programme were more important than the title. Had I given up medicine for such trivia?

ME: I still like 'Owl-stretching Time'. (*Of course, it was my idea.*)

T. JONES: Wheenh eheenh enehweech (*and lots of noises only the Welsh can make.*) I still like 'A Horse, A Bucket and A Spoon'. (*His suggestion.*)

J. CLEESE: Look, you Welsh git, we discarded that about two hours ago.

T. JONES: Fucking hell. (*Throwing papers to the floor.*) Aren't we able to *talk* about things?

J. CLEESE: Yes, but do we have to go on and on and on about it in such a high pitched voice?

T.JONES: Wheennh, wheenh . . . (J. CLEESE *guffaws like a barrister having made his point. This winds* T. JONES *up to near violence.*) Of course I go on and on about it. It's fucking important.

J. CLEESE (*patronizingly*): Terry, would you or would you not say that the rest of us have already agreed that we don't like it?

A heavy glass ashtray is flung across the room, narrowly missing J. CLEESE. *Characteristic of his temperament,* T. JONES *calms down instantly, having vented his spleen on inanimate objects.*

G. CHAPMAN: I still like 'Owl-Stretching Time'.

M. PALIN: No, I've gone off that a bit. I prefer 'Sex and Violence'. But I do think Terry's got a point about 'A Horse, A Bucket and A Spoon.'

J. CLEESE: Oh come off it. . . .

And so, it was decided to call it *Monty Python's Flying Circus.*

The BBC thought it was getting another in a long line

'Owl-stretching Time'

of unsuccessful, late-night, ex-undergraduate 'satire' shows. They were trying to find a successor to *That Was The Week That Was* then, and they still are. We didn't know what we expected to give them until we'd written it, but we knew that we weren't giving them 'topical' jokes, spoofs on political leaders or trenchant vignettes about life in North West One (London N.W.1). We were fed up with the traditional, well shaped 'sketch', the beginning, middle and the inevitable punch line. We wanted to be free to hang on to an idea for just three seconds or a whole half-hour if we felt like it. Despite its faults, the BBC hadn't succumbed to timid vapidity in those days and gave us a series of thirteen programmes to do, without demanding to see a script or a pilot programme and very gradually they even allowed us to do more and more outdoor filming. The style, if there is one, developed because we were the people we are.

Ian McNaughton, a tousle-haired loopy Scottish person was to be our director. Ethanol was a common bond between Ian and myself and I also liked his knack of getting things done while surrounded by apparent total chaos.

'Let's have a drink, hen, y'know what "a" mean? – Jesus Christ, they might grumble but we get twice as much fuckin' usable film in the can in a day as moast o'these other BBC pawnaggers . . . doan't ye think so Graham?. . . .'

' "A" do. Let's have another.'

'Aye.'

The meticulous, orderly side of John Cleese's nature – the side that counts how many 'O', 'A' and 'S' levels and what sort of a degree a person has got, as in some way definitive of that person's all-round ability, was uncomfortable with some of Ian's character traits, particularly Ian's friendliness which made John freeze and resort to schoolmasterly sarcasm. Terry Jones wanted to direct everything that Ian was directing, but Ian was very tolerant and I really feel that Ian never got enough credit for his part in the creation of *Monty Python's Flying Circus*.

For the first filming session that we ever did for *Python* we went up to Bradford in Yorkshire. Why? We didn't know then but we now know that Ian had a sure-lay scrubber of a girl-friend tucked away up there for his delights. As if that weren't enough, he booked a Soho stripper called Cecile Mould, whose naked top-half we needed in a newsagent's shop scene due to be shot some time later in London. However, Cecil Mould accompanied us to Bradford. We searched the script for the part Ian could have had in mind for her. This was not to be found and he was heard continually re-assuring her that she would be used the *next* day.

A most peculiar lady, with excessively large breasts, which on close inspection to my trained eye, had a series of half inch barely visible scars around the periphery of each para-boloid protuberance. This to me was evidence of some early form of surgical cosmetic 'enhancement', the injection of sil-icone quite possibly, most of which, on palpation, would have appeared to have hardened somewhat over the years, giving one the sensation of cushions firmly filled with gravel, making her surname curiously apt. These scars, she claimed, were the result of an occurrence in a night club when she had had the misfortune to trip up and fall bosom-down into a tray full of empty glasses – the glasses presumably being arranged with surgical precision.

Unfortunately for Ian, Miss Mould was not a man's woman. I first noticed this while travelling back from some filming in the minibus with her. While I was delighted that she had placed her hand down the front of my trousers and I, settling back and anticipating an enjoyable fondle, screamed out at the sudden pain occasioned by the nipping together and tearing of my prepuce by the said bitch, Ms Mould, who subsequently, while we were changing back at the hotel, caught Terry Jones with a similar playful blood-letting 'tweak' on the left nipple. Suddenly the reason for Ian's scars became more apparent and he, too, was anxious to send the lady back to her natural habitat.

The next day the camera was set-up in what passed for one of Bradford's night spots, complete with vomit in all the basins in the gents' loo. This was not a pleasant place to be at nine o'clock in the morning. The cast of *Monty Python's Flying Circus* sat around in assorted costumes while Ms Mould's strip act was performed with the highly improbable excuse of 'Well, hens, eh, we can use it as a link p'raps – know what "a" mean?'

Fortunately it was all over in time for her to catch the 10.30 train back to London.

Filming was always short sprigs of activity and large vacuoles of waiting around. Thoughts of sub-atomic particles occupied many tedious long waiting around bits. I wondered how many million neutrinos were zapping straight through my head at light-type speed every micro-micro-second.

I considered the neutrino. A particle having no mass: neither a positive or negative charge, just a characteristic spin, consisting of nothing else whatsoever.

Thinking of muons and quarks I invented the 'gluon' or at least sub-atomic particles of adhesiveness I termed 'fettons'.[1] I thought of the 'quarm', a particle consisting only of reticence and the 'giglon', whose elusiveness to sub-atomic physicists gave birth to the Big Laugh Theory of the creation of the universe.

A Quite Embarrassing Moment

We went away for a couple of weeks to do some filming for *M.P.F.C.* in Torquay. I stayed in the Imperial Hotel. The hotel that we'd actually been booked into by the BBC was the one that John Cleese was later to turn into *Fawlty Towers*. The owner of this particular hotel did not like guests and even thought that Eric's football gear, which was in a bag, and which Eric had just left outside the hotel, was in fact a bomb. He was completely round the twist, off his chump, out of his tree. I found the hotel intensely disagreeable in that it was absolutely impossible to get a drink. To make matters worse, they had a bar which could only be open while the owner was around, since he did not trust any of his other two staff. The bar was only open during the serving of the evening meal; the only person allowed behind the bar was himself and, as he was totally occupied supervising the serving of the food, getting a drink was out of the question. It was impossible as a place for me to stay. Cleesie also moved fairly quickly to the grandeur of the Imperial Hotel.

This was at a time in my life when I didn't think I'd been

1. Submitted in an essay to the Royal Society, February 1971 and rejected. (*See* page 69, Footnote 1.)

to a town until I'd actually managed to score with one of the local inhabitants. It was fairly easy in Torquay (in fact it's remarkably easy anywhere – praise be). I just went along to the Rockingham Club where there seemed to be several possibilities. I was soon chatting to a very pleasant group of people which included one very particular young man, an attractive black guy in a wheelchair. Carlisle was about twenty-five years old and had become a total paraplegic after breaking his back in a riding accident. He'd been quite an athlete prior to this, getting a great deal of attention from the ladies. He was also a very intelligent and sensitive person. He said that his relationships with women had curiously always seemed less than satisfactory and he couldn't quite understand this until after his accident while in hospital, where he found the attentions of the male nursing staff more pleasing to him and in fact had taken quite a fancy to one of them. He was now living with a good-looking young antique-dealer, Roger, who cared for Carlisle with genuine love and affection.

Carlisle was studying psychology and I suppose, having had to face such a huge personal calamity, then to be rewarded with a truly magnificent friendship certainly gave him great personal insight and a feeling for others and what motivates them. I chatted to him about his medical condition a little but mostly we had a good laugh, trying to imagine what was going on in the heads of the other people in that club. Why all that provincial reticence? They were all thinking the same thing – what a pity they couldn't get things together. The two of us being in a good mood tried, by making ourselves look idiots, at least to bring one or two of the peering, timid wallflowers to speak to each other. During this I found one wallflower – reasonable enough to look at but a bit plump in the face, who would do for a first night in Torquay. I've forgotten what his name was, but I'd never forget Carlisle. . . .

The second night at the Rockingham I really did find someone that I thought was fantastic, a real peach, and had a wonderful time. We exchanged telephone numbers but I wouldn't be able to see him again until the end of the week because he lived in Paignton with suspicious parents and had an unsuspicious girlfriend who had to be taken out. . . . At the end of that week the Python group decided it would be a good idea to buy an excellent dinner for as many of the film crew as we could muster at the Imperial Hotel, as a gesture of thanks for all they had done. There was, I must admit, a small feeling of guilt on my part, having lived in such comparative luxury. So it was arranged that a table for twenty-four people was to be set for us in the middle of the huge Grand Dining Room, a Very Imposing Room with its Magnificent Chandelier and other brochuric artefacts.

Now I wanted to show off. I'd been bragging a little to the others of my conquest earlier in the week, how fabulous this young man was – 'Cor what a little raver, a peach,' I'd say to M. Palin, T. Jones, E. Idle and J. Cleese, only to boost my own ego and make them, and particularly T. Gilliam, envious (*See* 'T. Gilliam and the Why Not Club, Munich', in *A Liar's Autobiography*, Vol. VIII). So I rang the peach up and invited him to dinner that evening at the Python table. He agreed and I was delighted, thinking of the night ahead.

The other Python people arrived and the rest of the crew all gathered and I was waiting in the foyer not far from the dining-room, hoping he would remember what I looked like and still like it and desperately trying to make myself look as obviously Graham as possible, though slightly more attractive. About twelve minutes later I was beginning to get a bit worried that he would not show. By now all the rest of the group were gathered round the table and were beginning to think about ordering.

Into the foyer came a black man in a wheelchair. It was Carlisle and I was pleased but surprised to see him. We chatted about this and that until he said how kind it was of me to invite him to dinner: it was obvious to me only now that I had, in fact, rung the wrong number. I was then left with no choice but to take my guest into dinner and so, taking over from the porter, I pushed Carlisle into the Grand Dining-Room, across the Grand Dining-Room floor with its Magnificent Carpet to the Entire, Magnificent and Grand Centre Table. The whole group at the table, noticing my 'peach', thought something. The air oscillated with boggling minds. Some didn't know where to look; some did. Whatever it was, they certainly thought that I had surpassed myself this time. I have never seen quite such a look, even on John Cleese's face, as was there at the moment we arrived at table. This, my close confidants must have thought, was the peach I was raving about the night before. There was nothing I could say to disabuse them of that. There was *nothing* I could do at all, in fact, there was nothing I *wanted* to do. I began to enjoy the situation immensely.

Carlisle was in splendid form. From the looks on several faces he knew he was the object of intense curiosity. He sensed mental turmoil. A wink and broad grin from me told him everything. Quickly realizing he had the entire table at his advantage he said to them, 'I don't know any of you apart from Graham of course (a wink); I haven't *met* any of you before (a grin), but, just as a game, let me try to guess some of your personality traits – let's see how many I get right!' He then proceeded to do just that with remarkable accuracy around the table. Carlisle was quite a hit that evening. I thought with tremendous internal glee of the tumult going on inside the heads of some of the more bigoted crew members. Whatever they thought at first, they were all thoroughly entertained and impressed by Carlisle.

I saw Carlisle again a few times after that, rare occasions when he and Roger came up to London. He was always an extremely happy person to be with but he knew his condition severely limited his life span. He was constantly getting a recurrence of urinary infections; nevertheless he took a leading part in organizing and competing in the Wheelchair Olympics. He died; but, just as people of his stature can, he left a lot of his mind around. What he was certainly affected my attitude towards people and to life. I'm sure he must have changed many other people too.

I had a mad year which I shall never forget, in which I wrote, or co-wrote thirty-seven half-hour T.V. comedy scripts. That may seem a lot and in fact it is, so you'll have to forgive me. There were thirteen *Python* programmes, for which I was writing with John Cleese; a series of thirteen for Ronnie Corbett, for which I wrote with Barry Cryer; and eleven episodes of *Doctor At Large*, which I wrote with

Bernard McKenna. But of course the really heroic part is not the sheer number of scripts but what Bengalis call 'Kwalitee',[1] and I will have to leave it to more modest people than myself to deny that all thirty-seven were reasonably good.

I went to one office for Barry Cryer in the morning, to another in the afternoon for Bernard McKenna and then spent the evening writing with John Cleese. Everyone, apart from Barry, thought I was being lazy. It was fun and I was pissed most of the time. I had to be because of the sheer strain of it. Much of that tightly-pissed period is still a binful of blurred memories.

The years that followed remain so similarly – which is an excellent excuse for a few disordered snatches. Extremely heavy petting in the back of a taxi-cab with four Chinese 'friends' reached a climax as we drove through Swiss Cottage towards Belsize Park, a mere prelude to a night of Neronic concupiscence.

Keith Moon and I went to meet Harry Nilsson at the Mermaid Theatre where Harry's *The Point* was playing. In the crowded bar, at Harry's request, Keith's 'minder', Richard, demonstrated his 'art' by kicking a cigarette out of Harry's mouth. You would have missed the action in half an eye-blink. The only man who could successfully wrestle a tank full of sharks who'd missed lunch, he is still a very close friend of mine if anyone is thinking of suing me. . . .

A Cambridge University Union debate where I made my point as a guest speaker by appearing dressed as a carrot and saying nothing. Ariadne Papanicolaou, the President, did not find this witty.

Possessed by the same urge to do exactly the wrong thing at Queen's University Belfast, I found myself launching into an Ian Paisley impersonation. 'Smash the Papist Swine with the Iron Boot of Protestant Enlightenment' I bellowed, before hiding under a table. . . .

I also remember waking up on the floor of the first-class

1. There is no English equivalent for this colourful oriental usage, meaning literally 'quail-ness'. Quails in Bengal are a great delicacy so an object of great 'Kwalitee' is equal in value to a large number of quails. The nearest English idiom would be 'good-thing-ness'. But that does not quite catch the suggestive essence of the original.

lounge of a Boeing 747 at 35,000 feet, not knowing how I'd got there – where I was going to, or where I'd come from, and not caring.

But all that is so much hot air behind the fridge. . . .

'Behind the fridge?' squawks Lady Bracknell.

'Oh come on,' hisses George Bernard Palin, 'We're still waiting. . . .'

But my mind is elsewhere. . . .

CHAPTER NINE

Brendan and Jimmy

I had spent most of the morning trying to explain the meaning of the word 'door' to a pretty young member of the Workers' Revolutionary Party[1]; nothing complicated, just the word 'door', as used in the context of departures. She, it appeared, was an out-of-work but rich young Hampstead actress, who had a real feeling for the person at the pitface. Her empathy for the working person had come to her in a vision she sustained during a two-week starvation-course at one of England's most expensive health farms near Redgrave in Dorset.

At first I was thrown by the novelty of such a pretty young slip of a thing expressing intelligent and earnest concern for the welfare of the masses. I was actually considering matrimony, until I realized that she had just explained for the third time how our so-called Socialist government was in fact a Wily Fascist Dictatorship; bugging their telephone-calls (you could tell

1. A recently formed Trotskian-Marxo-Lenitic-Kierhardoid-Sarahbern-hardital cahoot.

because whenever you spoke to another party member there was always that feeling that you just *knew* that someone else was listening – why else the ominous absence of tell-tale clicks?); obstructing their arrangements for meetings by failing to allow them to use Wembley Stadium free of charge; but, worse than that, constant prying (a landlord they had had under surveillance had almost certainly been seen sieving through one member's used cat-litter for Marxist microfilm). In short, one no longer had the individual freedom to plan a society in which such bourgeois concepts as privacy would be smashed.

I began to feel that she had been sent by some Outside Force to teach me the meaning of the words 'paranoid schizophrenia'. I explained, as charmingly as I could, that I thought she was a stupid little rich girl, while pushing her finally through my hinged barrier of wood.

David had sensed a nutter as soon as she walked in. He had wisely spent the morning making artichoke omelettes, and gave me an understanding grin as I bolted the door. I gave him a hug, and, as I tasted the latest omelette, he poured me a gin and tonic and we stared through the kitchen window at the sky over Hampstead Heath. Our home had survived another invasion; we were lucky; we could take on anything together.

'Ah! What a waste of a morning,' I said. 'Perhaps I can get down to some work now . . . I'll just nip down to the Monarch and meet Bernard. We've got to finish that *Doctor* script this afternoon. Back at half two.'

'Half three,' said David.

'No, I really am determined to make an effort today . . . half three at the latest.'

'OK, see you later.'

'Bring! bring! bring!' hazarded the phone.[1]

'It's all right,' I said, as David motioned me not to answer it. 'It's not the Workers' Revolutionary Party . . . Mmmm? . . . Yes . . . Yes . . . Well, we do need a new cleaner. . . . Three mornings a week . . . Hang on a moment.'

I put my hand over the mouthpiece.

'David, there's this man from Radical Alternatives to Prison who's been given my name by the Gay Liberation Front. Apparently there are two Irish boys, been in Ashford Reformatory

1. See note 1 on page 137.

awaiting trial, they were caught in the Isle of Man with a pair of knickers stolen from Woolworths, they were out of work and had nowhere to live. Apparently he's managed to find accept-able accommodation and a job for one of them, you know, so that it would be dealt with more like petty theft rather than some sex-crime, and he wondered if we could find a job for the other one.'

'Well, we do need a cleaner,' said David.

'So I'll say yes? Twenty pounds a week for three mornings?'

'Right,' said David, 'they can't be any more weird than the others we've had. That's a good idea, that's a much better way to help people.'

I agreed, and the man on the phone sounded very grateful.

I picked up *The Times*[1] and loped off to the Monarch with a 'that's the way to do it' kind of feeling towards the Workers' Revolutionary Party.

The Monarch was a splendid pub in Chalk Farm run by an exemplary ex-tank-driving Jewish matriarch. While she was engaged in sweet-talking a previously ranting methylated-paddy to the street you could ask her: 'Hey Romi, 23 across: "Grasp receipt and eat for a change – 9 and 6"?'

' "Cigarette papers" – easy. Now don't bother us again until you've had that cut seen to – have you got 14 down yet?'

'Not yet.'

'You're not likely to – it's "Panariste" – one of the King of Antioch's wives' waiting-women – bit unfair that one. Right, same again for everyone?'

Well, all we've written today is:

'INT. HOSP. CORRIDOR. DAY

ENTER PROF. LOFTUS.

PROFESSOR LOFTUS (brusquely): Morning . . .'

said Bernard McKenna. 'So we'd probably better be going after the next one after this.'

Writing afternoons often started like this – a few drinks over *The Times* crossword, followed by a few drinks and then an exhausting workout on the pinball machine with a few drinks, then a few drinks afterwards. That particular week we were at a difficult stage, trying to write the eleventh episode of a series of thirteen half-hour situation comedies – *Doctor at Large*. Not

1. Which I take for the crossword only.

inspiring the white heat of creativity that lends itself to a half a shandy and a cheese sandwich. In fact we were two weeks late in the delivery of that particular episode and the day before we'd even tried seeking sanctuary at our local church (thinking that Humphrey Barclay, a then TV producer, would not dare to challenge its sanctity). It was locked and shuttered. We shouted through the letter-box. This produced no reaction – except from passers-by. Pity. Could be one of the Church's few remaining useful functions.

At that time the Gay Liberation Front had begun its struggle against sexual oppression: men were up in arms to be arm in arm, women wanted to be fathers and the other way round; closet doors were blasted off their hinges and I had bought them a defiant tea urn for their meetings. Denis Lemon and friends also at that time[1] had held a meeting at my flat in Belsize Park which was the beginning of *Gay News*. I myself was going through a Militant Homosexual phase. An ordinary pub in Chalk Farm seemed like a sensible place to be wearing flowered shirts and pink trousers like a badge. And a badge.

Later that evening the pinball still attracted us more than the script. In the middle of getting my highest score of the day I overheard a remark from some people at the bar. The word 'Jessie' had been used. I looked over and saw two Glaswegian-style football supporters talking to a 'local'. I walked over to the bar, excused myself for intruding and told them that I was a homosexual and didn't much care for sniggering snide comments from ignorant people. Perhaps I could tell them a few things about their misconceptions. My friends at the pinball table stiffened, sensing imminent violence. Number one Glaswegian stared straight into my eyes and I stared back. After a long pause in which a fight to the last cell between his excitatory and inhibitory neurones hung in the balance, he said, 'That was fuckin' brave, that.'

'Not really.'

'No. That,' he repeated to his friend, 'was fuckin' brave, you know just to say that, like that, and that. Fuckin' great. I mean he didna know us, we coulda fuck'n killed 'im – 'a mean, what you havin' mate?'

'Well I was just leaving . . .'

1. And not earlier. See 'earlier'.

'No come on, Jimmy . . .'

Everyone else in the pub agreed with my new friends that I had been 'fuckin' great', sensibly preferring agreement to having their mouths filled with Caledonian forehead.[1]

The next day Bernard and I had got as far as:

'INT. HOSP. CORRIDOR. DAY.

ENTER PROF. LOFTUS

PROFESSOR LOFTUS (brusquely): Morning Matron . . .'

. . . when we were sidetracked by the thought that if you used the word 'bedpan' it always brought gales of laughter from the older ladies in the studio audience. We had resented this easy laugh in other people's episodes and decided to put it to the test and so an old X-ray cupboard became an old bedpan-cupboard so that the word could then crop up regularly without trace of subtlety or humour. (The experiment was disappointingly successful; the artless bedpan got the laughs every time.) We were writing about our sixth or seventh gratuitous 'bedpan' when, 'Bring bring bring,' insinuated the telephone.[2] It was the man from Radical Alternatives to Prison ringing to say the job for the other lad had fallen through, could I employ both of them for a short time doing the same job?

'Yes, provided it's for a short time and they'll only get fifteen pounds a week each, OK?'

The man said, 'Yes, that sounds good,' and went back to the courtroom. About an hour later there was another call to say, 'The accommodation for one of them has fallen through.' So I said, 'OK, we've got a spare room, we can put him up for just a couple of weeks.'

'Oh that's fine, we'll easily find somewhere else in that time.'

I should have predicted this, but half an hour later the phone told me, 'The accommodation for the other boy had fallen through.'

'All right, they can share the same room but the accommodation is just for two weeks and no more.' I was guaranteed this and went back to the task of gratuitous bedpan-inserting.

The two lads, because of my generous help, had been given a year's probation, said the next phone call and Mr 'Thing' would be bringing them round on Wednesday. They didn't appear on

1. 'A moothfull o'heedies.'
2. See note 1 on page 137, if you really must.

Wednesday. I was certainly apprehensive about what I'd taken on but two weeks and a part-time job for one of them was really all I had promised. I wallowed in the thoughts of how good I was being.

Mr Thing arrived on Friday with Brendan and Jimmy. I found out later that the reason for the delay in their arrival was that they had been taken to a hotel and he had been trying to screw them. Not knowing this then, I merely thought Mr Thing to be an over-talkative, mild man of about sixty years with a rather shabby raincoat. Brendan was a shy, pleasant and quite intelligent Dubliner. Jimmy was a loud-mouthed chatterer with buck teeth and an adenoid-pum-melling-Brooklyn-Irish-high-pitched-blackboard-scraping whine. To love them equally as my brothers was going to be a tough one. They both told stories of Ashford which were horrific. They and a friend called Charlie were the subjects of a half-revealing *Sunday Times* enquiry into that 'Reforma-tory'. Their experience with Mr Thing hadn't shocked them; they had learnt to expect that sort of thing as part of everyday life and were even grateful to him.

They were both particularly anxious to please us, as they told me this was the first time anyone had ever done anything for them without expecting something in return. They were keen to fit in and were soon hardly as noticeable as having two adolescent mentally deranged wild female cougars about the place and after a while intermittent high-pitched macaw-like screaming and the banging and crashing of favourite objects became acceptable background noise.

Jimmy came from Chicago actually, the 'Brooklyn' bit I mentioned was added because it was the most appalling nasal accent that I could think of at the time. He had been to Dublin on holiday with his family and there met Brendan while 'trolling' on the Quays.[1] The two had formed a friend-ship which made them inseparable. They had no sexual inter-est in each other but they seemed to like the same sort of man despite the fact that, being Catholic, they expected to get married and have lots of children. Back in Chicago, Jimmy had forged his father's signature to a cheque which paid for his return trip to Dublin. The two of them had left Dublin

1. The Quays in Dublin were then a popular meeting place for gays.

and set off to see if the streets of anywhere else were paved with anything else. A sensible thing to do: ignorance and poverty breed brutality and home life for both of them had meant being on the receiving end of anything from promises of eternal damnation to being held down by your older brothers to have the backs of your legs beaten with fire-irons.

The matron from a local runaway's home rang me to say that she had no room for either of my two lads and what did I know about Mr Thing? She had dealt with him before but recently had begun to suspect his honesty – did I know, for example, that he claimed to be my co-author on my next Monty Python book? We both came to the conclusion that he was an outrageous con-man who spent much of his time hanging around juvenile courts 'helping' youngsters to his own Radical Alternative to prison. . . .

David, Brendan, Jimmy and myself, realizing that help from outside sources was unlikely, decided that the two boys should stay until we could find reasonable accommodation and that they should both look for jobs – we really did only need one cleaner three times a week.

I trusted them and they never let me down. David and I left them alone in the flat for several weeks while I was film-ing in Munich and came back to find everything in order and a huge 'Welcome Home' sign in the main room.

Life for them was a fantasy and they regarded truth as relative and not absolute[1]. It took a great deal of patience and a lot of shouting to impress on them that they were on pro-bation and that they had enough money not to try to cheat London Transport of 10p merely because they had thought up a story which seemed plausible to them. Stretching David's tolerance to the limit, I took them on holiday with us to Ibiza. I warned them about staying in the sun too long and how dangerous it is to go to sleep on a lilo. Later that day I had to swim half a mile out and then another back, pushing a lilo loaded with a barely conscious Brendan.

We returned to our villa to see Jimmy who'd had to stay in, having turned lobster-red the day before (despite warn-ings about the sun). He was wearing a white sheet and was paddling around with mysteriously bright orange hands and

1. They had a point.(D.) Absolutely. (G.)

feet! I racked my brains for the differential diagnoses for orange extremities but came to the conclusion that a bottle of ManTan hadn't had its label read. They were trouble. But then so was I.

In a restaurant above the steps leading up to the castle (fortified part) in Ibiza town, a friend of mine who'd had quite a lot to drink started to argue with the bouncer. I joined in on his behalf, standing up telling the bouncer that if he wanted to push anyone around perhaps he should pick on someone his own size. He did. One big push. I'd forgotten that my seat was on the edge of the parapet and I remember falling through the air thinking, 'I wish we had the cameras rolling – I'd never do a stunt like this again . . .' before landing fifteen feet lower down on the stone steps going, 'Waaaghh . . .' I broke three ribs and was sore about the hips and head for a day or two, but as soon as I felt well enough went straight back to shout abuse at the man from a safe distance – no sense in calling the police to your aid in Spain in those days. . . .

Living with Brendan and Jimmy was rather like having two people around who were rehearsing to be Laurel and Hardy; the epitome of Murphy's Law[1], anything that could go wrong for them did. This brought out a paternal instinct in me and a 'They've got to go' instinct in David.

David was right: they would have to live their own lives – I think they had learned as much as we had time to teach them. After sporadic attempts to hold down jobs, Jimmy managed to get one on the London Underground. He was very proud of his uniform, which he regarded as the first step towards his ambition of being an airline pilot. No longer on probation, Jimmy moved out and lived at a friend's flat. Brendan stayed on several more months until he found a flat which was suitable for both of them. Brendan came back to Belsize Park three times a week to do the cleaning as originally planned.

I was very pleased with the progress they had made, particularly Brendan, who was quite literate. They both took

1. Which states that in a given situation anything that can go wrong woll.

pride in what they had achieved and even invited me round to dinner at their place. I recognized quite a lot of my own cutlery, plates and dishes but I kind of assumed that they knew that I knew I would have wanted them to have them.

Then Jimmy moved out of their flat to live with a new friend but made frequent visits to see Brendan at work at our place. Suddenly these visits ceased. There had been a quarrel.

A month or two later Jimmy arrived at the flat one night very drunk and with a slashed left wrist. I examined this, cleaned it up and it didn't look too bad. No severed tendons. I put a temporary dressing on it and tried to persuade him to go to hospital for sutures. He refused. Eventually, with Brendan's help, we persuaded him to go for treatment. The cuts were not so deep that further surgical treatment was essential but I was aware of the psychiatric implications and did not want to bear that burden alone. . . .

I assumed that this half-hearted attempt on his own life was a cry for the attention his new friend was not providing. Brendan and Jimmy saw each other again and for a time all was well.

Jimmy by now was working in a pub. One day his new friend came to see him there near to closing time and an argument flared up. Jimmy rushed off in a fit of pique, expecting to be followed by a contrite friend. He ran home to his flat and decided to stage a little display, just to show how deeply he had been offended. Jimmy's idea of that kind of display was to hang himself from a clothes-line post in the garden, while standing on a chair waiting for his friend. Unfortunately he didn't realize how fatal hanging actually is: the chair slipped from under him and he died. Either the chair slipped by accident or he was stupid enough not to know that your head doesn't like being without a blood supply and that he thought he could hang dramatically there until his friend came home. . . .

I hate to think of that struggling figure trying to tear the noose from his neck that he had put there himself: there were two noose marks, one on the neck, the other across the face at chin level and scratch marks suggesting he'd tried to wrench it upwards in his struggles to pull the thing free.

The coroner rang me up, as I had been his employer for

A dingy drawing-room

some time. He didn't need any further verification of identity and I was glad I didn't have to see the corpse. Now I had to tell Brendan about the death of his friend. He took the news deceptively calmly but insisted on going down to see the body. I told him not to go – it's pointless – 'He's dead isn't he? That's it. What you will see will not be Jimmy. It will be a horrible sight.' I knew, I had seen hangees before – the bloated, blue face etc. He went anyway, and found the sight indeed horrific, feeling, I suppose, some guilt himself because of their recent argument and long separation. He projected most of that guilt onto me.

For a period of six months or so after that he would ring up drunk in the early hours of the morning blaming me for killing his friend. During these calls it gradually became apparent that really he was punishing himself. Getting drunk every night didn't provide any relief. One night he called and simply said, 'I'm in an awful place, get me out of here please, Graham.' I took a mini-cab round to the address he'd given. There were sounds of a party of sorts in a basement flat. I went in and there was a room full of middle-aged men sitting around in a tiny dingy drawing-room watching a teenager dancing around in his under-pants. I saw Brendan, he was very drunk – I strode up to him, lifted him up bodily and carried him out over my shoulder. The next day we had a chance to talk soberly at last.

Brendan had a sister in Eire to whom he had written frequently and we both felt that some time away from London would be good for him. He went back to Ireland and from his telephone calls it was clear that he had managed to overcome the negative aspects[1] of his feelings after Jimmy's death. He had found a friend there who said that there were good prospects for work in Denmark and that was where he was going.

He has written frequently since from Denmark and has a steady job, a flat, friends and can even speak the language.

I have tried to write this succinctly without allowing too much emotion to cloud my account of the events and so would like to end by simply screaming, 'Waaaaaaaaaaaaaaa aaaaaaaaaaaaaaaaaaaaaaaaaaaaaaaaaaaaaaaaarrrrrrrrrrrrrrrrrrrrrr rrrrrrrrrrrrrrrrrrrrrrrrrrghghghghghghghghghghghghghghgh ghghghghghghghghgh!!!!!!!!!!!!!!'

1. A psychiatric way of expressing unbearable heartache.

CHAPTER TEN

John of the Antarctic

One January night in 1972 I lay languidly draped over the comfortable deep red Chesterfield. I listened to the tiny clangs as bubbles of carbon dioxide effervesced their way past my ear to burst at the top of a quadruple glass of ginandslimlinetonicwithicebutnolemonin. I relaxed in the sheer lack of austerity in this, the largest room in my penthouse in Belsize Park. Banks of spotlights focussed harsh geometric slabs of magenta, emerald green and beige across the walls while from a thurible effused frangipani, bergamot and chypre, compounding a mirantic furlor of didantillism. From some forty feet away I could barely make out the distant drone of my brother, who is, after all, a surgeon examining a friend of mine. This friend had an umbilical hernia I thought needed attention. His examination complete, my brother agreed and

173

we set about making the arrangements for his admission to hospital.

This particular friend in need of surgery was also a heroin addict which slightly complicated arrangements in that we had to make sure the hospital fully understood his need for large quantities of opiates. He had been treated for his addiction by methadone substitution but lapses were frequent and the only constructive thing I'd been able to do for him was to show him how to shoot up properly and give him a liberal supply of disposable syringes and needles, which would at least minimize the trauma to his veins and exclude millions of nasty bugs from his bloodstream. He was to be cured of his addiction a year later while working in Germany. He was discovered to be addicted and they treated him harshly but effectively by immediate complete withdrawal. The efficacy of this cruel but dangerous regime I was later to bear in mind during my Chapter Nought days. . . .

But to return to the point reached earlier in this chapter, my brother and I had now just finalized arrangements for his hospitalization when the telephone rang and a voice said, 'Is that Dr *Graham* Chapman?'

'Yes,' I riposted.

'Ah,' said the voice, 'you're just down as "Chapman, Dr G." in the book, I just wanted to check. I've got a young man staying who's quite ill. He's got a high fever but he refuses to go to a hospital or see my doctor. He says that he's met you. You gave him your autograph once. He says he would see you.'

'Who is that?'

'You wouldn't know if I told you but it's Richard Milner.'

'You were right,' I told the voice and that the best thing would be to wrap him up well, and bring him round, as we seemed to be holding a mini-surgery at my flat that evening anyway. Half an hour later he arrived, a good-looking young man, introducing himself as John Tomiczek. I had seen him outside a Kensington restaurant, the long dark hair, olive complexion, bright blue fur-lined jacket and blue and maroon trousers jogged the memory. I showed him into the main room and took a brief history. He was seventeen years old; from Liverpool and in London staying with a friend

A mirantic furlor of didantillism

while waiting to take up some sort of apprenticeship with a shoe firm. He had had two similar attacks of fever at roughly monthly intervals but this was the worst yet. He also complained of tiredness, general muscular pains and headache.

My brother examined him and finding enlargement of the superficial lymph nodes considered glandular fever (or infectious mononucleosis, if you prefer, though why you should I don't know), the most likely diagnosis. The fever at monthly intervals sounded more ominous, however; reminiscent of a Pel Ebstein fever found in the more serious condition of Hodgkin's disease (lymphadenoma if you prefer that!) We decided immediate hospitalization would be wise and with the aid of his Efficaciousness A. R. Bailey, Physician, had him admitted to the Royal Northern Hospital for bedrest and the appropriate clinical tests.

The tests confirmed the diagnosis of glandular fever and showed that he'd had a fairly severe infection which had affected his liver.

Two weeks later the ambulance service rang me to say, 'We've got a John Robert Tomiczek here who has only given us your address – since you had him admitted, where should we take him?' They actually sounded busier than that.

'Bring him here,' I said, thinking, 'Well, we can sort everything out between ourselves. . . .'

John arrived and certainly looked better, though still pale and weak. We had a spare room now that Brendan had left and since John was rather non-committal about this friend he'd been staying with, Richard Voice, I thought that, rather than have him going off, popping into pubs, doing further damage to his liver, perhaps a short convalescence with us would be wise.

I asked him about his family and background but because of his strong Liverpool accent and an ability to feel less well whenever he was questioned I let things ride, thinking, 'Well, he'll tell us when he's ready. Meantime, we shall make sure he eats well and continues to recover.' This proved difficult in that he only ate fish and chips and jam 'butties'. But four weeks later he had indeed recovered. . . .

I had just finished an intense writing stint and thought that a weekend away would be a good idea and so it was that

David; Andrew, my Irish-Portuguese chauffeur; John and I set off to go to North Wales. I had equipped all of them with climbing-boots, anoraks etc.: at last I had a team who would come climbing with me.

It was an uneventful journey apart from a major accident when a twenty-five-ton truck drove into the side of my Vanden Plas Princess at 50 mph[1]. Fortunately the car bore the blow pretty well and we were able to continue our journey. There were two doors on the other side of the car, after all. Rather later than I'd hoped that night we checked in at the Pen-Y-Gwryd Hotel at the foot of Mount Snowdon. . . .

It was February and Snowdon can be a difficult proposition in the winter but we were well equipped: ice axes, ropes, carabiners, space blankets, emergency rations – the lot.

The next morning when we set out from Pen-y-Pas there were patches of blue in the sky and the air was crisp. Up above us Crib Goch, the first peak in the Snowdon group we were about to climb, stood covered in cloud down to just above the snow-line. We would have at least a thousand feet of snow and ice to tackle before reaching its summit. From Crib Goch I was hoping to complete half of the Snowdon horseshoe by going onto the top of the highest peak and then make our return to base, coming down via the easy Pyg track.

I think John was a little alarmed at the number of people he saw coming down having failed to get up: I was slightly apprehensive myself but confident that this was nothing four fit young men couldn't take on. . . . At one point there was a tricky little slab of rock covered with ice, which in the cloud gave the appearance of being steeper than it actually was. John was worried at this at first but I lowered a rope to him to make sure that he got up safely. We very rarely needed to cut steps and made good time up to the summit itself.

The ridge extending from Crib Goch to the main body of Snowdon is a narrow one and in these conditions represented a knife edge of rock covered with ice; steep snow slopes fell precipitously on either side disappearing into the cloud below. It was appallingly cold; way below zero and the wind tore at us, showering us with spikules of ice. . . .

1. Actually it was 40 . . .

Suddenly everything went crimson with little gussets of gamboge, but Evans knew what Scott was thinking: 'That bally man Oates has been a pain in the neck ever since we hit Antarctica nine months ago. The frost over Evans' eyebrows and icicles in his beard can't hide the fact,' thought Scott, that Evans' lips, though green with cold, would if they could, have said what he knew him to be thinking. Oates was a bore, an unmitigated crushing bore; whatever possessed them to accept such a fellow in the first place. 'Well, he's nipped out for one of his boring little walks. He'll be back in a minute, screaming odes at us at the top of his voice over the howl of the wind.'

The two men stared at each other, then, acting as two men, crawled out and dismantled the tent, ran off and piled it onto the back of the sledge. The sledge, covered with bodies of the dead dogs whom they later intended to give a decent English burial, was heavy, but the thought of Oates quoting 'a thing of beauty is a . . .' made them pull even harder and they broke into a jog as the thought of Oates' premature return struck them both. . . . Soon they were miles away, safely encamped again, making up stories about how brave Oates had been, 'walking out like that, saying, "I'm just going out for a walk," though really we both knew he now considered himself a burden on us.' Tee hee hee, they both thought until they didn't. . . .

. . . Almost as suddenly, everything went white and we were progressing along the ridge, for safety in the high wind quite often sitting astride it, with one leg hanging either side. We were getting along; slowly but safely and I was thankful for the cloud; if any of the party had seen the drop each side they might have been as worried as I was.

We came to the end of the first part of the ridge and the going became easier but I thought we'd better abandon our original plan and get down sooner. I was thinking of safety and the pub opening hours.

I decided to take a more direct route down a gully to our left. To make a quicker descent I unroped the whole team for the climb down the snow slope. John, thinking, 'What a relief, it's all over, we're down the dangerous bit,' leapt off ahead. I stopped him and we all roped up again. I knew that steady progress was better than haste because at the bottom of these couloirs what in summer is a waterfall in winter becomes a miniature glacier. Sure enough, when we got down to the point where the waterfall should have been there was an ice floe. . . . I had to cut steps down it carelessly.[1] It took about an hour and a half to get down the ice slope but as soon as we were at the bottom of it we were almost on the snow-line: scattered patches of snow and rocks above a scree.

On easier ground again we unroped. We could actually see the Pyg track three hundred feet or so down below us. John again set off rather too quickly and I shouted at him to slow down. Unfortunately he'd picked up so much momentum he couldn't stop, tripped and somersaulted about thirty-five feet down the mountainside. In the process he cut his forehead and collected some chest abrasions and a possibly fractured left leg.

We climbed down to him and tried to carry him but the pain from the leg was soon too much for him to bear. I stayed with him, wrapped him in space-blankets and patched up his forehead with surgical tape, sending David and Andrew down with our map reference to get the mountain rescue team.

The weather was too foul for the helicopter to fly and so we had to wait for the R.A.F. mountain rescue team to come on foot. Even though we were much lower down the mountain than we had been it was still extremely cold and by now darkness had fallen: a high wind and driving snow enhanced the sense of danger.

I had a torch and a whistle and began S.O.S. signalling but John and I had to wait there for four hours before any sign of rescue. Another party, loosely fitting our description – two men, one young, with a broken leg – had fallen lower down the mountainside. The R.A.F. picked them up and thought they had rescued us. They hadn't.

The team arrived back at base and there waited an anxious David and Andrew. 'It's OK, we've got them,' said the R.A.F. David, looking at the faces said, 'That's not Graham

---

1. Carefully.

and that's not John either.' The R.A.F. team set out again, with David showing our route of descent.

Four hours at minus temperatures in the dark somewhere on a mountainside is a bit telling on the spirit and strength. John wasn't too bad, as some other climbers had stopped on their way down and provided extra blankets. I was worried. I continued blowing my whistle and flashing the torch at intervals, as you're supposed to, and waited for a return signal. Wonderful. I heard their whistle way below and to the left of us. I increased my blowing. A marvellous moment this: I heard a distant shout – they must have seen my light. I saw their light quickly return my flash. That was fanbloody-tastic. F-bloody-anta-bloody-st-bloody-ic. All thoughts about what Eternity smells like had vanished.

They climbed up to us and gave me some hot soup as John was carefully strapped onto a tubular alloy mountain rescue stretcher. Then we had to lower him down the mountainside. Quite a big team is involved in these kind of operations – you have one person going down in front to work out the best route, a couple of bearers at the front, three either side of the stretcher and a team of about eight others hanging onto ropes behind so that the stretcher can be lowered down crags and cliffs.

Being a non-injured party I was naturally expected to help and so took my place hanging onto one of the ropes at the back. I was so exhausted I couldn't help for long – my hands couldn't grip any more and I kept stumbling. The last three hundred feet down were too much for me. I gave up and said, 'Sorry, I can't help any more,' and slid down the rest of the way on my arse; I couldn't even walk – it was appalling.

Once the stretcher-party reached the footpath they set off at a quicker pace. One of the R.A.F. team stayed with me just to make sure I didn't stagger into the lake which was almost as exactly near 0°C. as you can get without water being ice. The unfortunate thing was that what is normally a causeway across the lake, Llyn Padarn, in the winter isn't: it is four feet deep in ice-cold water, either side of which, should you step off, is forty feet of ice-cold water, which isn't good for anyone's health. Either that or you go round the lake, a four-mile slog. I didn't want to go four miles, as opposed to a hundred yards, neither did the man with me. But we had to cross that lake guided only by the lights of the Land-Rover on the other side. It was pitch black and if we'd slipped off on either side we'd both have been dead – no doubt about it. We got across, up to the waist, in my case, in ice-cold water, at the end of what had been rather a long day. (David had by now crossed it three times. . . .)

We arrived back at the Pen-Y-Gwryd and John was taken off to hospital. We discovered that all the residents had been listening to the rescue on short-wave radio because the owner of the hotel, Chris Briggs, used to be a mountain rescue organizer. His hotel, after all, was the base for the training of the Everest team. We got back there to, well it wasn't thunderous applause, but it was a lot of interest because they'd been listening to the mountaineering drama in progress. The rescue team had no time to receive 'thank you' drinks: they were already out scouring the peaks for three more missing climbers.

Anyway John had been taken off to Bangor hospital and David, Andrew and I felt we deserved several pints of beer and quite a few scotches, a meal and more scotches, only to be rung up at about 11 o'clock by Bangor hospital who said that the young man called John Tomiczek was refusing to stay in hospital. I asked them about the X-rays, whether they'd X-rayed his head because of the injury to it. They had; no signs of damage and his leg had only a hairline fracture. I thought, 'He's had a hell of a day anyway and obviously wants to be with his friends.' I told them, 'Send him round to the Pen-Y-Gwryd Hotel and I'll do a head chart on him, we can have him back to you in twenty minutes if anything goes wrong.' This meant checking his pupils, pulse, blood-pressure and breathing-rate regularly. So, after all the exertion that day, I had an alarm clock brought to me and got up every half hour to begin with and then every hour to check all those physical signs.[1] It was an exhausting process but all was well.

The next morning the local police came round to the hotel wanting to see me and asked, 'Who is this John Tomiczek – what do you know about him?' I told them the story of how I came to meet John and how he came to be with us. They

1. Except the blood pressure. I'd somehow forgotten to pack a sphygmomanometer. . . .

then said, 'What would you say if we told you he's fourteen years old and has been missing from home for nine months?'

I said, 'I'd tell you exactly what I just have – that's what happened.'

If it had not been so, the word kidnapping would spring to mind but I'd been trying to find out where his parents were etc. etc. . . .

What had happened, of course, because of the routine police check-up on the mountain rescue, was that they had actually found out his home address; his father was coming to collect him. . . .

He was a bit late in arriving. It's not far from Liverpool to the Pen-Y-Gwryd – about a two-hour drive, but his father took five. I thought, 'If that was a son of mine I'd have been there in a flash.'

But after I had queried his delay with a raised eyebrow, John's father and I got on very well. We both came to the conclusion that if he were taken back to Huyton, Liverpool, he would only run away again. John's mother had died some five years ago and his father had four other children to look after on his own. A proud man, understandably he did not want institutional care for them. John had been asked to leave one rather strict R.C. Grammar School and was a persistent truant at another. We asked him, 'Would you go back to school if you stayed in London?' 'Yes,' said John. So informally he became my ward and I his guardian.

An odd feeling, suddenly becoming the 'parent' of a teenager. All my paternal instincts emerged. My experiences with Brendan and Jimmy had shown me that this behaviour pattern was innate: suddenly it was exactly as if John were my son.

Before returning to London John went to stay with his father for a couple of weeks. We were going to Jersey to do some Python filming and John arrived back in London in time to join me on that trip. I was very pleased to see him; so was David, so was Brendan. Our flat was his home. Brendan and he even built a new cage for our white mice.

The local nick, the Hampstead nick, rang that very morning and said, 'We'd like to have a talk to you Dr Chapman, about the John Tomiczek business.'

I said, 'Oh. Oh well, all right.'

'Shall we come up to your place?'

'No, no, I'll come up to the police station, don't worry.' I told them. 'As it happens, John's here at the moment, he's just arrived.'

'Is he? Well you'd better bring him too.'

John and I both went up to the police station. We had about three hours before catching the plane for Jersey and we were kept there for two being questioned, John being rather more fiercely interrogated than I; after all I was a doctor. A rather nervous Sergeant Greene of the CID, the Hampstead perverts branch, was questioning me. Eventually he plucked up courage: 'There's one thing I do have to ask, Dr Chapman.' After a long pause, 'Are you a homosexual?' I said, 'Yes.' He was expecting the more convenient answer, 'No,' and then everything would have been all right. We would have just gone. But, having had several articles published in which I stated that I was a homosexual, I didn't feel I could say 'No'. And I couldn't honestly say 'No', anyway, but they obviously had to check to make sure nothing was 'going on' between John and myself.

They then tried to get in contact with his father and eventually reached him by telephone and said to him, 'I gather you've given permission for your son John to go to Jersey with Graham Chapman.'

His father said, 'Yes, that's true.'

The police then said, 'Did you know that Dr Chapman was homosexual?' and he said, 'Yes.'

And there was nothing they could do, 'much against their better judgement'. We just caught our plane to Jersey. . . .

It may surprise the police but I happen to believe, along with every homosexual that I've ever met, that it is anti-social and insensitive in the extreme for anyone, of whatever sex, to attempt to force any sort of physical attention on another person. . . .

John had found a stable, happy home and soon had a circle of friends at his new school. Apart from my being a bad influence, in that my drinking habits encouraged him to drink too much at one time, I think David and I have done a pretty good job. We're very proud of him.

CHAPTER ELEVEN

A Chapter of Violence

A girl styling herself 'Miss Finsbury' rang to ask if I would help her charity by drawing the raffle at an old folk's evening festivity. The old folks were in for a treat; a pantomime performed by locals, followed by a raffle drawn by someone they'd been told was a celebrity and then a cup of tea and some biscuits afterwards. All I had to do was draw the raffle, it sounded simple enough so I agreed to Miss Finsbury's request.

The day arrived and I went to Finsbury Town Hall. There were a lot of old-age pensioners watching a pantomime and a very beautiful creature wearing a sash with 'Miss Finsbury' written on it introduced herself as Anna, last year's Miss Finsbury. She was more attractive than most beauty queens I had seen and had obviously done a bit of homework on me – she had a secret stack of cans of lager – the only other refreshment available being tea. I downed a couple of cans and distributed the prizes at the raffle with great speed and in a loud voice, hardly giving the old folks time to ask, 'Oo's 'ee?', then went back stage for a few more lagers while the organizers 'pushed' the tea and biscuits. It was all very simple and I had a very pleasant chat with the extremely pleasant and intelligent Miss Finsbury.

A couple of weeks later she rang me up again saying that this time there was another similar charity function that 'I thought would be more entertaining' because it was a disco-dance for younger folks. All I would have to 'do' would be another raffle. I said, 'Yes, fine. Where is it and how would I get there?' She said, 'Don't worry about that, I'll pick you up on Tuesday' – the whatever it was.

Around about eight o'clock on Tuesday-the-whatever-it-was, along came Miss Finsbury with a somewhat older lady and I invited them in for a drink, before setting off to the large pub which was the venue for this disco evening. I turned the football on the television off, saying it didn't interest me as I used to play Rugby and I remember the older lady saying that in her opinion Rugby was more of a *man's* game than the rather namby-pamby football and expressed interest in broad shoulders and meaty thighs. She could possibly have been Miss Finsbury's mother but I didn't ask. The two were in definite agreement about men. After a few gin and tonics, John, myself and the two ladies set off for the pub somewhere on the North Circular Road. Miss Finsbury was delightful company and we chatted happily on the way there and when we arrived the disco was in full swing in the large room at the back of the pub. After a few drinks I got up onto the stage and did the raffling. Because the raffle was for an old folks' charity I'd bought quite a few books for the raffle and so had John. He finished up winning two of the main prizes. That was my work finished for the evening and so I told Miss Finsbury I'd see her at the bar and buy her a drink.

At the bar with John I was trying to get the attention of the waiter. The man standing next to me said, 'I'll get these, Graham.' I looked at him. He was about six foot tall, I suppose – wide, not fat but definitely wide and solid – the sort of figure that reminds me of a Victorian door, strong, tough and not to be thrown about lightly.

I said, 'No, thank you very much, I'm getting a round for someone else.' I noticed that just behind him stood a slightly

'I'll get these, Graham.'

smaller person who nevertheless reminded me of the sort of man who could well have been a middle-weight boxer – not particularly huge but power-packed. This man said nothing but seemed to be very definitely with the man who looked like the Victorian door.

'No, no, no,' said the Victorian door. 'I insist, Graham. What do you want?'

I said, 'A large Gee and Tee for me, same for John, oh and I was getting a Bacardi and coke for Anna, you know, Miss Finsbury.'

He ordered the drinks and said, 'It's only fair for me to get the drinks, you've done your bit for the evening haven't you?'

I thanked him and insisted that I should get the next round. He then, with a slight but definite 'loom', said in a very measured voice, 'You like Anna, don't you, Graham?'

I sensed some other meaning behind this but, being innocent anyway, said, 'Yes, yes, I like Anna.'

Had the man grown? He certainly looked larger. . . . 'I thought you did,' he replied quietly, weighing the effect of each word. 'She's a nice girl.'

'Yes, she is a nice girl, very, very pleasant. . . .'

'Well, you'll be needing *this*, then,' he said and out of his inside pocket he produced the thickest bundle of ten pound notes I'd ever seen.

I said, 'What's that?'

'It's a thousand pounds for you.'

I said, 'No, it isn't.'

'Yes it is, Graham. Go on, keep it.'

'What for? It's got nothing to do with me.'

'It's yours isn't it?' He looked even larger. . . .

'No it isn't, I haven't done anything to earn it.'

'It's yours, keep it.' His silent friend's taut muscles rippled visibly.

'Look, I really don't want it, thank you very much, I earn my own money. What I did this evening was for charity. I don't want it, thank you very much.'

'Well, you'll be needing it now, won't you?'

'No I won't.'

'Oh yes you will.'

'Why, why should I need it?'

'Well, you'll be looking after Anna now, won't you?'

My brain reeled. . . . 'No, no I won't be. No, no I won't be looking after Anna.'

'You like her don't you?'

'Yes I do like her but that's all, I've only met her once before this evening.'

'She's talked a lot about you, Graham. Go on take it, you'll need it.'

'No thank you. . . .'

Still the boxer-looking gentleman behind said nothing.

'Here have this, then,' he said as he brought out another wad of notes looking exactly like another thousand pounds. 'Go on, it's yours, put it in your pocket, just take, it's yours.'

I don't know why but something somewhere in the back of my mind told me that if I accepted this money I would be admitting guilt and that somewhere later in the evening my throat could have been pulled out. Maybe the back of my mind was exaggerating but I wasn't taking any chances. As firmly as I could under the circumstances I said, 'I don't want any of your money thank you very much. Now let me get you that drink. I've got to go very soon.'

I tried to order a round of drinks from the barman but he had already begun to pull down the iron grid at the front of the bar to close it. I pleaded with him through the descending shutter, 'Could we have just one more quick round, please?'

'No, it's well after hours, we're closing.'

'Please, just one more won't hurt.'

'No, we've shut.' Clang.

The door-like man then said, 'Don't worry Graham, I'll fix it,' and disappeared through a door at the side of the bar. A few moments later he came back and so did the barman. The barman looked very pale and trembled as he fumbled with the latches and bolts opening up the bar again. The bar was open again and orders were being taken. The middle-weight boxer stood there and still said nothing. We exchanged pleasantries about the entertainment business and that evening in particular and how nice Anna was to involve herself in charitable works. . . .

On the excuse of going for a pee I managed to nip off and find Anna behind the stage and said, 'There are a couple of people I'm a bit worried about out there. You did promise that a taxi would take me home afterwards. Could you please order a minicab now and tell it to come round to the back of the pub not the front? Please could you do that for me quickly?'

She said, 'Yes,' she understood. She thought she knew who the people were that I was talking about and she would arrange everything – no need to worry, just leave in ten minutes out of the back of the pub. I felt relieved and went back to finish another drink with them, and saying, 'Well I have to be going now, nice to have met you both, cheers, all the best . . .' John and I walked off, slipped through a door at the back of the stage and went out to the back of the pub.

There was a waiting mini-cab. I glanced in at the driver and said, 'Hampstead?' He said, 'Yes,' and, looking over our shoulders John and I climbed into the back of the car.

My heart skipped a beat or two.

Reclining against the upholstery were the man that looked like a door and his friend that didn't speak. The door man, whom from now on we might well refer to as 'Trevor' said, 'Hello Graham, we've got to go back through your part of town. We thought you might like to stop off at a little place for a drink, like.'

'No, no, I'm very tired, I'm just going home to Hampstead, perhaps another time.'

Trevor said, 'No, it's a great little place – not too many people know it, just one drink eh, Graham?'

I began to have visions of a quiet little place that we could be taken to where one could be nailed to garage doors and have one's head screwed to a coffee table, or perhaps one's legs stapled together – that sort of little place.

This particular evening I hadn't been drinking very much (for me) – I'd had a couple of little smokes – and, considering the situation in which I now found myself, I remained relatively calm. I insisted that this cab was going to Hampstead to drop me off at my house. The cab driver now joined in and said, 'Yes, Hampstead, that was the job, that's where I'm going. If you want to go anywhere else, get another cab.' He said this in a rather tremulous voice. I think he didn't want to be a party to any nailing to garage doors or screwing to coffee tables that might have gone on later in the evening. He obviously knew the two people in the back of his cab and was scared.

But Trevor continued to insist that we go to this quiet little place he knew. I thought that, rather than the quiet little place Trevor knew, it would be wiser if I invited them round for a drink at my place. At least that was my territory. I knew where there were telephones. There were neighbours and there was also an ice-axe behind the door in a cupboard near the stairs. It seemed to me that there were better opportunities for survival in my own environment. They agreed to this, at least, when I say 'they', Trevor agreed and the other gentleman said, 'Mmmnn!' The other gentleman, it now became clear to me, had previously restricted his conversation to grunts because he had no tongue. I assumed that this had probably been removed because of some indiscretion earlier in his life. I didn't care to question Trevor about it at that particular moment.

We drove back to my place, the fifth floor flat in Belsize Park. We arrived outside the block of flats and left the cab and Trevor told the cabman to wait for them. This was encouraging. We climbed up the stairs and went into the flat and I began to pour them some drinks in the kitchen. Trevor now explained to me that Miss Finsbury's husband was 'doing' some forty odd years inside one of Her Majesty's Prisons for causing grievous bodily harm during the course of an armed bank robbery and that he, Trevor, was the man designated to look after Anna – make sure no harm came to her – if I got his meaning. He'd formed the impression I'd been seeing rather a lot of her. I explained that I hadn't and he seemed to accept that for a moment or two.

Trevor and I had a long conversation in the kitchen, the details of which I shall give in a moment. Meanwhile John spent his time with the man with no tongue in the main room. The man with no tongue was trying to explain something of what was going on by writing notes on the only available piece of paper, one of John's history text books, the appropriate portion of which I hope you will see reproduced on this or another page.[1]

1. We've put it on page 192, squire. (Printer.)

It seemed that the boxing gentleman would do anything for Trevor because he had once saved his life when they were both in the Merchant Navy. His tongue had been removed because of something he'd rather not write about. He said that he liked John and myself and was a bit concerned for my welfare, because Trevor sometimes went a bit too far. Seeing John's concern about this he wrote, 'DON'T WORRY ABOUT TREVOR HE BAD IN THE BRIAN. IF HE TOUCH GRAHAM I KILL HIM.'

Meanwhile in the kitchen, I was rapidly coming to the same conclusion, namely that Trevor was completely out of his brian. A possible psychopath; a large one and certainly not to be trifled with. I remembered watching a psychiatrist friend of mine, Dr Robin Anderson, dealing with a paranoid schizophrenic who went completely 'gaga' one evening in a Hampstead restaurant. This particular person, a London School of Economics lecturer, suddenly loudly proclaimed that he was worse than Hitler and would shoot the balls off all the students who were fucking his wife. He said he had a gun in his brief-case and would shoot everyone in the entire restaurant. Robin dealt with this very well. The restaurant had quickly emptied of everyone, of course, apart from ourselves. By talking to the man and asking him why he thought he was worse than Hitler, he immediately involved him in some detail he felt obliged to explain. This had the effect of keeping him off 'boiling point'.

I tried to take the same kind of interest in everything that Trevor said in the hope that he wouldn't become possessed by the red mist of rage. . . .

'You like Anna, don't you Graham?' He was beginning to grow larger again. . . .

'Yes, I do like Anna.'

'She's very nice, isn't she?'

'Yes she is very nice'—

'Only she belongs to someone else, like. . . .' He couldn't have looked larger.

'Good, yes.' I was sure she did, good-looking woman like that.

'I'm kind of, like, her old friend, you know. I'm looking after her.'

TREVOR SO KIND BUT
HE LOST HIS CONTROL

I CAN TEACH HIM
A GOOD LESSN

TREVOR IS ALWRIGHT.
HE IS A NICE MAN, HE
IS JUST A BIT ANGRY ABOUT
SOMETHING. I DONT ~~to~~
KNOW ~~the~~ WHAT.

'Yes, yes and very well too, jolly good. Would you like
another drink?'

'Have you *had* Anna?' I couldn't move.

'No, I haven't. I told you, I've only met her twice, once at
the old people's thing and then again this evening, that's all.'

'Yes but she came up here to the flat *didn't* she?'

'Yes but with an older woman, who, I think, was her mother and they can't have been here more than half an hour.'

'You were a bit late arriving at the pub.'

'Were we? We stayed here for half an hour. Look, I did not touch her. I haven't *had* her. She's very beautiful and I could be tempted but I've told you the absolute truth.'

'Yes I'm sure you have, Graham, yes I'm sure.'

'Look really, if you don't believe me – Look, I'm a pouff.'

'Don't give me that, mate, so am I. I think we both know that doesn't change anything, does it, *Graham*. Now about you and Anna. . . .'

There seemed to be very little way out. He was convinced that I had done something. However, I was convinced and correct in saying that I hadn't. This kind of conversation continued for some time with as many diversions interrupting his line of questioning as I could possibly throw in. I placed a great deal of faith in him being convinced by the truth. I also had a strange inner calm that could possibly be attributed to the 'joint' I'd had earlier, but we were now beginning to assume an almost doctor-patient relationship.

I was certainly taking the whole thing more calmly than I would ever have thought possible in the circumstances. At the end of yet another prolonged interview even Trevor seemed to think that I had been telling the truth. John and the gentleman with no tongue rejoined us and everyone appeared to be reasonably happy. More drinks all round. John and the tongueless middleweight played a noisy game of 'football' on a machine we had in the hall. I had a particularly irritating neighbour downstairs who throughout the day used to annoy me, since I worked at home, by knocking down walls and rearranging the interior of his flat, making a terrible racket. Anyway this evening, like many others, the mild little man came up to complain. He rang the doorbell, I opened the door.

'Excuse me, I hope you realize it's 12.30 at night and there is rather a lot of noise.' He'd hardly finished saying this when the gentleman with no tongue grabbed his head and Trevor rammed the door shut on his neck. . . .

Now that we were all friends I felt braver in their company

and managed to calm down Trevor and his friend. 'It's all right, he's from downstairs, he means no harm, don't worry,' I said, prising the door open and allowing Mr Black-and-Decker to pull his head back out of our door. I went outside and explained to him.

'Mr Black-and-Decker, I sometimes do have some very odd people in my flat. Sometimes it's part of my work; I enjoy having odd people around. This time it isn't. These are the oddest and certainly the most dangerous people that I have ever met. I advise you to go downstairs and treble bolt your door and say nothing.' He, quaking as he was, shivered his way downstairs and did exactly that. I thought it wiser not to make any suggestions to him along the lines of ringing the police. I had no wish to be misinterpreted by my 'guests'. That incident over, I went back in.

The game of football was finished. John had made the mistake of winning but fortunately the gentleman with no tongue was a good sport.

Trevor then said, 'Graham, can I have a word with you?'

'Yes, sure,' I said, thinking perhaps of one more interview in the kitchen.

He said, 'No, come in here.'

'Where?' I said.

'The bathroom.'

'All right,' I said, fearing I didn't quite know what. A pretty horrible but a strangely distant fear. I was no longer really afraid; I suppose it's a kind of dull acceptance that if something really fearful is about to happen and is unavoidable then it's unavoidable, so why get excited about it? So I went into the bathroom. There, terrifyingly, predictably, while holding his empty glass close to my throat, twisting it round as though preparatory to plunging it through my carotid artery, he said, 'Graham, tell the truth. Did you have Anna?'

'I've told you, *no*. I met her twice. Once with the old people, once here tonight for half an hour with the older woman and at the disco, that's all.' The glass twisted round two or three more times. He glared at me. Days passed. He finally saw that I was telling the truth and put the glass down. 'Well, let's have one more drink then we'll be off.'

It seemed as though the ordeal was over. We had a drink

and I went to look out of the bedroom window to see if the cab was still there. It wasn't. The driver wanted no part of the evening's business. . . . I told them that the cab had gone. Trevor swore a bit and said, 'Don't worry, we'll get home all right.' I told them I'd ring for a cab for them. There was a minicab firm just down the road that I had an account with and they'd be around in five minutes.

'No, no, don't worry about that, Graham.'

'No, it's easy, they know me, no problems.'

'Don't bother, the police will take us. . . .'

'What?'

'The police'll take us.' He smiled.

'Look, I'll ring for a cab.'

'No, Graham,' and he lifted up the receiver and dialled the police station and said, 'Hello, this is 14 Denham Court, fifth floor flat. There's a geezer 'ere runnin' around with a knife. No, no I think you'd better come quicker than that 'cos he's got this other geezer out on the balcony.' Click! The receiver went down. About a minute and a half later the doorbell rang and there at the front door was a uniformed sergeant and two plain clothes detectives. The detectives seemed to recognize Trevor and his friend and walked straight into the flat. I stayed to talk to the uniformed sergeant who'd been told firmly to wait outside. I said to him, 'I don't know who these two men are but, whatever you do, please could you get them out of my flat.'

Meantime the two detectives had joined Trevor in the bathroom where, coincidentally, they were overheard by John who'd gone for a pee in the bog, next door. The gist of the conversation was that Trevor would give the two police-men £250 each, if they would drive him home, which they agreed to. The two detectives left, saying everything was all right and Trevor and his friend left waving a cheery goodbye.

There seemed little point in reporting any of this to the police. Clearly some of them knew already. I accepted the whole deal on Trevor's terms, and have never seen or spoken to Miss Finsbury again. Really, honestly, I haven't!!! . . .

CHAPTER TWELVE

The Hardrock Café

Paul McCartney had just formed a new group called Wings, and they were making their UK debut at the Hardrock Café in Piccadilly, an excrementally trendy hamburger joint. One of George Melly's ex-wives/girlfriends/husbands/boyfriends rang and asked if I'd be prepared to compère the evening. 'This sounds interesting,' I thought, 'and not too taxing', as all I would have to do would be to announce the other acts filling in before the 'big' moment. I had never met Mr M. but had once sat behind him in a viewing theatre while listening to the music he'd composed for *The Magic Christian*. Here was an opportunity to meet the front pieces of the said Mr M., while engaged in good works. It was for the benefit of a group called Release, who dealt with the problems of that section of society who could afford to go smoking, shooting and sniffing certain substances. I was all in favour of this, as I've always believed that people should be allowed to do what they want with their bodies. After all, it's all they've got. I agree with the law that it is wrong for anyone to go round poking other people with sharp pointed sticks,[1] but if someone wants to poke himself with a sharp pointed stick, that's fine by me. They can go and batter themselves to death with huge lumps of poisoned granite for all I care. There is the problem of an over-populated world. . . .

The other point of course is tell someone not to do something and they're bound to want to. When suicide was illegal, it had a certain glamour about it, it was an act against society, against the law. Then someone apparently came to his senses, realized that there was no point in punishing a corpse, and the law was changed. The expected chains of suicide parlours did not spring up. Even the poor attempted suicides no longer found themselves hounded by the police or mentioned in the press, and so lost the attention they were in search of. Less important than a parking offence, suicide was dead.

This is a great shame. As a species, can we really afford not to have people committing suicide? If the law had any global conscience it would surely make suicide punishable by a fate worse than death, to enhance its popularity. In fact now that I've come to my senses on this issue, I realize I was talking nonsense about the abuse of drugs. They should be made *more* illegal – even aspirin and tea. At present aspirin kills an average of seventy million people each year in Northumberland alone. Imagine if it was made illegal – boy, what a figure! In no time at all we'd have the population of Britain down to two million or so, and be self-sufficient again, and no longer dependent on these wretched Arabs, d'you hear? And if the population fell below the optimal two million mark, sex could always be made illegal for a controlled period of time, till the required number was reached. . . .

I arrived at the Hardrock with Tom, my driver, and John. I was supposed to introduce the guest-groups to a crowd of rich pointless layabouts who were showing how cool they were by taking no notice of anything that surrounded them, including each other.

I have never since met such a concentration of undeservedly rich, immodest, exhibitionist, trendy, conceited,

1. Should they not want to be.

vacuous, mean-minded, illiberal, self important set of micro-cephalic twits. Neither would I wish to. They regarded themselves as something apart from mere mortals and should have been. Their twittering vapidities reached a noise level several decibels above the pain threshold of a Tyneside ship riveter. One idiotic son of a millionaire watch-salesman, who thought it was hip to spend his father's fortune on releasing Betty X, a convicted mass-murderess and racialist, had thought it amusing to bring his screaming one-year-old daughter to have her ear-drums pierced by famous musicians. I announced the first group. No-one was bothered, so I stood on an even higher box, had the sound turned up, and bellowed at them. Three or four people turned round, and the first set began. I can't remember their names – they were very good, and their loudness completely drowned the screams from the baby. The rest of the room was unaffected, surrounded by a sound-shield of self-importance. One or two of them may have enjoyed the music but were afraid to be seen doing so, in case it wasn't quite cool enough.

The next act was two topless go-go dancers. They were looked on as being uncool by everybody. That annoyed me. While the next group was playing, I overheard the girls talking backstage.

'I was so embarrassed.'

'So was I. Weren't they awful?'

'It's not that, dear. My son's headmaster was out there, and we've got to go out again – like this. I'm sure he recognized me.'

'I should think he was the only one that did. And if he's seen you once, what's wrong with twice? We've worked for weeks on this act and that snooty lot out there didn't even look. We might as well have had clothes on.'

I was pleased at finding two human beings in the place, and thought they deserved a better chance. Fifteen minutes later, before their next appearance, with a certain amount of shouting and a little pushing, I managed to clear a space on the floor for their act. All was ready and I was about to signal the girls to come out now that they were assured of at least some spectators. A tall, fat, black lady wearing a startling creation, now made herself apparent,[1] with her huge funnel of a dress in vertical black and white columns of ostrich feathers, complete with a high, arched collar fanning out some feet above her head made from the same pluckings. I had seen her earlier standing in a conspicuous part of the room looking as conspicuous as anything I have ever seen being ignored. Now she was making her final bid to be noticed; she pushed through the artificial cordon I had created and glid hippopotamously across the empty floor towards the bandstand, where she could have had no possible business. I asked her to move back; she continued her unpauntly progress. I asked her again. No response. I then gave her a playful tap with the side of my foot on her ample rump to attract her attention.

At this she spun round and bellowed, 'Get him, Cosmo!' A tiny Italianate creature immediately leapt at my throat with his fingernails. This miniscule fiend had come from nowhere but really knew how to dig his ample nails in. This was such a bizarre method of attack that it was half a second or one before I made any serious attempt to brush him off.

Now the bouncers at the club had been given strict instructions that at the first sign of trouble the person or persons causing it should be ejected. They wanted to make sure there was no trouble, after all it was the first appearance of Wings and, to be fair, looking at the crowd, I think it was a wise precaution. However, they assumed that, as I was twice the size of my assailant, I must have been the aggressor. They hadn't followed the proceedings well enough to recognize that I was in fact the M.C. I was grabbed firmly by two very large gentlemen so that I could no longer use my arms and I was carried outside. They made no attempt to dislodge the persistent Sicilian vampire during this, leaving me to shrug him off at the door. I still don't quite understand why they didn't remove him from my throat as they pushed me into the street. Cosmo was allowed to stay inside, where everyone had started suddenly to look at what was going on. Even the trendiest had cast an odd glance. Those peace-loving cool trend-setters homed in on the violence like Puritans on a knocking-shop.

1. Made herself a parrot? (D.) Apparent. (G.)

'Get him, Cosmo'

Tom, my driver, who had seen the incident from the bar, rushed out to help. I mopped up some of the blood on my neck with a handkerchief, told them I felt perfectly all right, and was ready to go back inside. I wanted to finish my job, and I wasn't bothered by a few scratches from a silly little man. The bouncers wouldn't let me in. I explained that I was the compère. But they were large gentlemen with tiny brains and hadn't been programmed with this piece of information. I asked to see the Release organizer. They'd never heard of her. I asked to see the manager. 'No.' I went through the whole explanation again, and then once more. 'No.' I gave up and was driven home.

The next day the organizer rang up to apologize. I told her I felt fine. It certainly wasn't her fault – you can find madmen in your own living room – and I didn't want to make trouble for her organization. I thought no more about it. Then a few days later large blisters appeared on the right side of my neck, from the jaw to the collar-bone, with the occasional unpleasant scab thrown in. Impetigo, I thought, and dosed myself up with ampicillin – a powerful type of penicillin. After about five days the mess had almost disappeared, but I began to wonder whether Cosmo had deliberately infested his fingernails with bacteria.[1] It's a strange way to attack anybody, though possibly quite common in Naples. A week later the wounds were almost completely healed.

I was glad about that because I was about to start filming a *Monty Python* television series. Unfortunately I made the mistake of squeezing a small spot above my right eye and very soon I had a very handsome set of blisters and scabs extending over the entire eyelid. The swelling caused a deficiency in the visual department. Thinking, 'Perhaps I'm not a very good doctor, really', I ran off to see the good Doctor Alan Bailey. He poured me a gin and tonic and I felt better already. He said, 'That looks pretty bad, old man,' and suggested large doses of intra-muscular penicillin: that is a syringeful into the bum twice daily. 'Oh shit,' I thought, 'the filming. I can hardly ask Alan to come round at 6 o'clock in the morning and 8 o'clock at night to stab me in the buttocks.' I said I'd do it myself.

1. *Streptococcus pyogenes.*

At 6 o'clock the next morning I tried to persuade someone else in the flat to do this for me, but there were no takers, so I filled up the syringe, wiped the position of my choice with surgical spirit, and stood in front of a large mirror trying to get a decent view of my rump. I held the syringe poised and thought for a moment about the plunging action about to take place. I put the syringe down carefully, and went and had a large Scotch. I'd given thousands of these injections to other people, and it didn't seem to hurt them. Then I remembered the last time I'd had an injection of penicillin: the sensation of the needle going in was nothing; but the sensation of the penicillin going in was as though I'd been given a present of 2cc of lead in the buttock. I went back to the mirror, looked at my eye and thought, 'Right!' A quick wipe of surgical spirit, then I thrust the needle in quite confidently. Well, it wasn't too bad. I pressed the plunger home. 'O-o-o-o-o-o-oh!' I removed the empty syringe, regained some professional dignity, and said to myself, 'There, it wasn't as bad as you thought, was it?' 'Yes,' said my right buttock.

The next two or three injections became almost routine. After that, I was beginning to think my right buttock was full, and had to move on to the left. This meant considerable gymnastic contortions.

The penicillin was effective, the impetigo soon threw up the sponge, cringing under the weight of the antibiotic attack. The few remaining penicillin-resistant organisms, if any, died of loneliness. But on the third day of filming we were on location in Ealing. I had run out of disposable syringes, needles and ampoules of sterile water. I waited for a break in the morning's shooting so that I could nip away for a few minutes to a nearby chemist. I had just finished some inane scene dressed as 'Mrs Entity' and there was a brief pause while the cameras were relocated for the 'Colonel' to say something. So it was that I walked into Timothy Whites, the chemist, dressed in carpet slippers, stockings, a print frock complete with false tits, a colonel's jacket, hat and moustache and asked for a supply of needles, syringes and water for injection B.P.C. The ladies behind the dispensing counter eyed me with ill-concealed boggles. The senior assistant pointed out that they could only sell such goods with proper medical permission. I quickly explained that it was quite all right and told them to look me up in the medical register. This she did and by now the entire staff were peering out from behind the shelves of pharmaceuticals to see the eccentric practitioner walk off with his 'Shooting-up gear!'

This should have been the end of the 'neck incident' but about a month later I received a badly-written letter on solicitor's note-paper claiming damages from me for a lady for 'scratching her chest, causing her severe mental upset and tearing a dress valued at several hundred pounds.' I sent a reply via my solicitor, the gist of which was, 'Piss off.'

I had plenty of reliable witnesses to the actual events. We heard no more except a 'rumour' that the lady had spent some time in the famous Hôtel de la Détention Policière (Femmes) somewhere in Paris. There'd been some kind of dispute involving 'dud' cheques being passed by the 'gallant duo'. . . .

CHAPTER THIRTEEN

A Python Stage Tour

The tour was going well. A success everywhere. I had pulled in South-ampton, Oxford and even Cardiff. I had expected Cardiff to be a bit of a challenge, but, full of gin and the feeling of superiority over mortals which commonly afflicts the adulated, I had reached my zenith in a naughty and, to this day, illegal act upon the floor of an empty dressing-room. The fact that this romance blossomed from love at first sight right through to mopping up in the ten minutes available between Acts I and II of *Monty Python's First Farewell Tour*, merely seemed like a good idea at the time, your Honour. . . . Pressure of work, previously unimpeachable character etc. etc. . . . Sorry, where was I . . . merely seemed to add piquancy to the occasion.

However, Sunderland was a toughie – only two entries in the *Gay Guide*, 'open summer, weekends only'. No point in even trying, I thought, on a Wednesday night in March. And so for the first time I went with the others to eat after the show. But I never felt happy in a place unless I'd scored. This thought nagged as I drank my way through the meal, and watched the others being interested in eating, chatting with wives and non-wives. I had more to drink, and decided to cross Sunderland off the map. On my way past the reception desk I said, 'Good grief, there's no one to go to bed with . . . where are all the young men around here? This is absolutely dreadful.' I went to my room and fell drunkenly onto the bed, alone.

I woke up at 5 o'clock in the morning to find the night-porter in bed with me, nude. He wasn't particularly my choice of person, but under the circumstances he was welcome. He had let himself in with a pass key, and, faithful to the hotelier's code, put customer satisfaction first. The satisfaction was mutual and I even found myself wanting to stay in Sunderland, because as things would have it, most of the junior staff apparently had a similar devotion to duty. . . .

After Sunderland we spent the weekend in Dallas, Texas, the birthplace of *Python* in the States. Odd that our television shows were first screened on the public broadcasting service of a town which was looked upon generally as 'a bit' right wing. We were there to assist in a fund-raising week for that particular TV station and I was there to get laid. This time I got lucky – with a Red Indian. After the glitter of the TV show it was 'Wham! Bam!' 'Straight-Back-To-His-Place', a ten-foot-by-six lean-to with good stereo and curious rats at the back of a garage in a part of town tourists don't get to see. Wonderful!

Back to the Tour of England: we stopped off at Windermere for a night on our way down south from Glasgow. A reporter did an interview with Mike, Eric and myself in my room. We all went out to eat but I got bored with eating: I wanted Sex! Sex! Sex! Walked halfway round Lake Windermere. Lifeless: not a soul. I went back to my room in the hotel to go to bed. There was a knock on my door. It was the interviewer.

He said, 'Sorry to disturb you, I seem to have left my microphone.'

I said, 'I bet you only did that so you could go to bed with me.'

He said, 'Oh all right.'

Whammo! Zap! There was no holding me now. Stark staring raving Mad.

New York was 'Fun City'. How about that time in Raffles' Bar – good-looking Puerto-Rican? . . . Vrooom! – Straight into the telephone booth with him. We didn't give a damn – we were young and in love. For three whole minutes we grappled with each other, but, out of concern for the other patrons of the bar we left the door of the booth open – if we'd closed it the lights would have gone on. . . .

Thirty-five thousand feet up in the air with an Eskimo in the toilet of a Boeing 74[1]. . . .

We left Sunderland far behind, and as our Range-Rover sped us on our way to Edinburgh at a cool 120 m.p.h. on the hard shoulder with hazard lights flashing, I handed the bottle of Glenfiddich back to the curiously pallid hitch-hiker, saying, 'I can't understand why nobody else is using this lane,' and marvelled at the splendid unpredictability of life.

In Edinburgh I was very naughty indeed. . . . Two young.[2] . . .

1. STOP! STOP! STOP THIS! Stop it! I've no idea which one of you co-authors wrote this. It is out of place, inaccurate and rather *strong*. Don't you think we should build up more steadily, from childhood sweethearts via light to heavy petting with girls, thoughts of marriage etc.? You know very well there's not a shred of truth in it; why should we take the risk of offending the vast minority of people who, quite justifiably, take offence at offensive things? (G.) Sorry! (D.)

2. I'm afraid I'm just going to have to stop this chapter. (G.)

CHAPTER FOURTEEN

More Touring

Throughout *Monty Python's* tremendously successful tour of Canada
my behaviour was exemplary.[1] I met
some delightful people and made many
friends, including some local dignitaries,
one of whom is pictured over the page[2]. . . .

Meanwhile a short time warp away the scene changes[3] to
Monastir, Tunisia, several years later the same century, about
teatime. I wander down to the hotel swimming pool, order
a Seven-Up, never expecting it to arrive, and lie down in the
fierce unrelenting sun next to the nude Brazilian lady with
the fierce, unrelenting breasts and write this in a book.

For eight weeks I am playing Brian and the Unit Medical
Person. Brian is the central character in the film and is

1. That's much more like it!
2. Excellent. I presume the picture you are showing will be the one of
me taken with the Commissioner of the Royal Canadian Mounted Police
in Winnipeg. (G.) You could be right. (D.)
3. Does it? I shall be keeping an eye on this, you know. (G.)

Graham seen here with the Commissioner of the Royal Canadian Mounted Police in Winnipeg.

involved in almost every scene, but it is the people round him who do the funny things and have the funny things done to them. I am trying to play the Unit Medical Person in much the same way. The first few days in Tunisia had their salt tabletic, Lomotilic and occasionally streptotriaditic moments, but were mostly spent being Brian. Work on the first scene started at 7 a.m. and took twelve hours in direct sunlight (it was 95°F in the shade at 9 a.m.) made hotter by two huge arc lamps directed straight into our faces. Add to

208

that the fact that this scene was being shot so that it would look as if it were taking place at night, and you have a disorientation and mental and physical torture not permitted in wartime.

I was grateful that for the first few days, rumours that I was medically qualified were treated with mild disbelief, and that I was generally regarded as one of the most unhinged of one of the world's maddest groups. My successes with the little pink tablets, however, were quick to blab and word got round that diarrhoea wasn't caused by the weather, nor was it an essential part of being in Tunisia. I was beginning to think things were a bit dull and was idly thumbing through some common need emergencies to refresh my mind on how to deal with such fascinating problems as embalming at sea, rabies in charcuterie accidents and medico-legal aspects of hired camel-bite fatalities, when I had to deal with a patient whose successful treatment established the Medical Person as being altogether a more important character than Brian.

He was a designer from the art department who had been ill since arrival. He had been seen by the local doctor and was getting worse. His girlfriend explained in pulverized English that the doctor had said that he had a virus in the tummy, a pressure of twelve (sic) and must eat only carrots and rice. He had been given intra-muscular aspirin injections by a friend of theirs who was a nurse but she, apparently, could not be found and the doctor was expensive.

I found my patient in a stifling, darkened room lying motionless, pale and staring blankly at the ceiling, prepared to join the choir invisible. My first thought was to nip back and read up on 'notification of death on a foreign soil', but in a lighter, breezier room he looked more like an ill, rather than a very ill, man of thirty-two. I was relieved to find that he could speak with difficulty. The difficulty – and the relief – being that on examination I found that he really had tonsillitis. Penicillin brought his temperature back to normal. A more varied diet and encouragement at the thought that the end was not nigh did the rest.

After that I had a regular evening surgery with 'on the set' follow-up clinics. I support Terry Jones in championing natural, unprocessed foodstuff when we are all safe in our aseptic isle, but I wished he would consider the Mediterranean as a sea processed by man's personal and industrial waste. Then perhaps he would have spent less time urging unit members to eat ethnic. And they would all have spent less time sitting in lavatories.

The Brazilian lady's breasts are still without relent but they have definitely shrunk – shrunk in comparison that is – with the smug, huge, crude milkers now surrounding me. Suddenly at the poolside the atmosphere is chill – as though a BBC TV interviewer was strolling casually up behind me, about to ask if I would mind if we would just. . . .

The Canadian tour over, I went for a few drinks in Los Angeles. I had been guided from the tiny forward drinking compartment of a Boeing 747 down a perilous spiral staircase into a coma which had been waiting for me on the tarmac. The coma had evidently whisked me to a room in what I knew to be a hotel . . . my house in Highgate had shoddy room service and fewer Hyatt ashtrays.

Several gin and tonics with ice but no limes in them later I was able to walk about as well as a newborn giraffe. A few more G and T's and I was steady enough to hold a glass and turn off 'Body Buddies'. Through the window I could see that I was no longer wherever I had been whenever it was. 213 area code meant Los Angeles and I rang down to the lobby to see if I had checked in and whether I was in a party or not.

'Er, Los Angeles,' I thought and ordered a huge limo. The driver demurred at first but then obeyed and we drove sedately to a restaurant I'd heard about. It was embarrassingly opposite to the hotel.

Sitting down to breakfast off nuts and gin I looked round at people lunching at other tables. One of them, who may well have been a scientologist, was rash enough to comment on my choice of breakfast. I dimly recalled uttering a few strange but applicable adjectives before and while being dragged up the steps and hurled onto the pavement. The novelty of being thrown out of an establishment *up* the steps made me forget to question why they hadn't thrown out the scientologist.

The limo driver, who had never liked the restaurant in the first place, warmed to me and wafted me off to a place he thought would suit my mood called the Polo Lounge. Looking around the room I must have had some uncharitable thoughts about how much the occupants cared about the rest of the world. I met a friend who seemed to have been made to feel ill at ease but after a few G and T's I grew expansive and felt fit enough to feign paraplegia.

The staff coped with the situation gracefully and only became slightly ruffled when I explained that my paralysis was merely a joke but one which nevertheless I was playing to the hilt. In no way was I going to move from the waist down and so a wheelchair was brought and, helped by my driver, who was enjoying himself and by the staff, none of whom were, I was scooped up and wheeled outside to the car. Here, overhearing a grumble from one of the staff, I ordered them to stop, fell over in the wheelchair, and dragged myself the last few yards, using arms only, into the back seat of the limo absolutely refusing help.

I went back to my hotel and changed my name at the desk. I had made a few enemies and one firm friend for life . . . the limo driver.

After a couple of days drinking in my room, Harry and Keith had to leave. As I was saying goodbye to them in the hotel lobby a Californian sun-chick, lissome, bronzed limbs, pert breasts and golden-flowing hair, said, 'Hi!'

I said, 'Hullo,' and asked Harry – 'Who's that?'

'I dunno, I thought she was with you.'

'Perhaps she is,' I said. 'Shall we go up to my room?'

'Sure,' she said.

My suite at the Continental Hyatt also contained my one-time financial adviser – Major Sloane. He was on the telephone in his own room and his eyes bulged as I showed 'Eve' through to my bedroom. This compelling lass carried a straw beach bag which, it transpired, contained a cerebrum-jangling eroto-pharmacopeia of unguents, oils and embrocations. My entire body was pampered; the scent of exotic oils hung in the air as her sensuous probing hands worked their magic. . . . 'That was fun,' I thought after Eve had finished

Gratefully using my telephone

having her way and had blown her goodbye kiss.

I relaxed quietly gulping at a gin and tonic and wondered if there were any more like her down in the lobby. . . .

Zoom.

In the lobby a young girl came up to ask me if there was another telephone in the hotel.

'Sure, use the one in my room,' I said, as I already began to propel her towards the elevator.

'But it's my mother who wants to use it.'

'Well bring her up too,' I said magnanimously. 'I don't mind if it's a local call. . . .'

There was no stopping me now. Major Sloane was still on the telephone – this time to one of his daughters, whose birthday it was. . . .

'That's nice dear, what else did Mummy give you?' – His entire head pucened and his exophthalmos worsened. . . .

As the Mother, quite unconcerned by the activity her daughter was engaged in, gratefully used my telephone, while in full sight of her and the 'bulging' Major Sloane, I pushed my rampant p. . . .[1]

---

1. AND THIS ONE TOO! You know perfectly well why. And don't think I didn't notice that offensive photograph! (G.)

CHAPTER FIFTEEN

Bavaria and Glencoe

The Pythons, as we now were, went to Bavaria to film two fifty-minute shows for German television. The first was filmed in German which meant most of us learning our lines phonetically – a very strange excursion. When we arrived in Munich the show's producer, Herr Doktor Doktor Biolek wanted to show us round the place in case any location sparked off an idea for the shows. Sitting in 'limos', traversing the ring road, going 'Ooh look' and 'Mmm that's interesting!', I was quietly into alpha rhythm looking into middle distance when suddenly I saw a road sign which meant something: Dachau 15 km. I persuaded the driver to stop and spoke to Dr B. They couldn't quite understand why we should want to see such a place but the 'group's' decision was that we should.

We arrived at the town and asked the way to the 'Kassette' – prison camp, which we knew had been preserved as a 'don't do it again' monument. The first two people we asked had no idea that such a place existed. The third, a younger woman did and quite unconcernedly gave us the directions. We arrived at

Dachau concentration camp at 5.15 p.m. The 'guards' were beginning to close the gates, it was due to close at 5.30. I shouted, 'But we're Jewish, let us in,' a jokey remark I wish I had never made. They allowed us in and, as soon as I walked through those gates on a wet evening in April, I could sense something quite horrific – the very earth was leaden, saturated. There was the feeling that many others had walked through those gates never to walk out, their only sin was being Jewish, homosexual, gypsy or tramp. There was a powerful presence, a heaviness of soul about the place. When will we ever learn?

In modern Munich there are copious naughty-niteries for a person with apparently perverse predilections, let alone alliteration. And when we returned to make our second epic – in English this time, to be dubbed later – I was not allowed to stay in the same rather nice, small family hotel because of my previous behaviour – our previous behaviour – David was culpable too. . . . On the last morning of our stay we'd left our room, looking somewhat post-orgiastic and had the effrontery to appear at breakfast with our two young gentlemen friends. This would not do. . . .

On our second visit David had not joined me for the first week of filming and so it was that I was taken to my hotel, one which Herr Biolek thought would be more suited to my taste. . . . The Deutsche Eiche (the German Oak) certainly was odd, and therefore was. It was a small and very old Bavarian Inn reputedly a haunt of Hitler and a few friends before their whole thing grew to World War II. It was now the haunt of different and altogether more harmless eccentrics – as some might think – gentlemen who liked dressing-up in leather and wearing motor-cyclic clothing were wont to meet there. The place was run by a wonderful matriarch and her equally gross and matriarchal son – the food was good and wholesome, the beer and wine excellent and cheap – the rooms spartan but clean and functional, functioning until all hours of the morning . . . it was best to keep your door locked unless you wanted visitors with extremely friendly intentions.

It was there that one afternoon I met a black American guy (it *was* during the Munich Bierfest) from the Munich cast of *Hair* whose eye caught mine and we whiled away an afternoon upstairs. . . . My description of his anatomy to Michael Palin later earned him the title of the 'Boston Startler'. I certainly, with all my background of rugby clubs, hospital wards and other more personal experiences, had never seen anything like it.

David was quite impressed with this story when he arrived. Another 'friend' I had made stayed with us for a night and I was woken by David gently nudging me over his sleeping form. He was pointing at the pillow. Next to our friend on the pillow lay a wig! The long-haired guy from last night had in fact closely-cropped hair! David said, 'Let's go to the bathroom and get up noisily and that'll give him time to get his wooden leg screwed on too!' We did and on emerging found him long-haired again. It was quite common in Munich in the early seventies for 'fashionable' young men to wear their hair short for work and long for the evenings out . . . we were nearly always discreet. . . .

We left Munich after a weekend of Octoberfest, about which I have a complete memory block, except that I know I woke up in my room with two young men and what felt like a broken shoulder – I could have fallen off one of the fairground attractions. I must have had a good time because I couldn't help grinning a lot.

We'd more or less finished filming and partly as an excuse to leave for London early I agreed to be the Python representative to accept the *Sun* award, the Television Trophy we apparently, although no-one was supposed to know, had won.

So David and I zoomed off to the airport – I hadn't had much time to down my early morning drinks and so practically threw up over the nice lady at the airport check-in, but we were soon through the barrier and I was happily drinking huge gins and tonic for breakfast. I had a similar lunch on the plane and then on the way from London airport dropped in at London Weekend TV for a few more drinks donating a large poster of a nude Nazi to the female catering-staff who were most impressed at the detail. . . . I arrived home in time for a few drinks before dashing off to the Dorchester Hotel where the awards were to be handed out.

We staggered into the hotel and asked a receptionist where the Telly thing was and she pointed to a room where we could see people drinking. I ordered a drink from the bar and was surprised when asked to pay for it and further surprised when I looked round the room to find that the only recognizable TV personality was Percy Thrower – apparently some Gardening Club was having a private function. This was not the right room.

We left and asked for further assistance. This time we were shown into the Grand Ballroom. Chandeliers sparkled everywhere, people were even wearing them – this was the correct venue for glitter and no mistake. The vast room was full of personalities seated at tables. I even recognized a few, and we were guided to ours to be told we were rather late for dinner but they would see what they could do. Luckily we'd brought our starters through from the other bar and helped ourselves to the ice bucket.

The awards ceremony was to be televised, that much was obvious from the cameras and Pete Murray on the podium preparing to M.C. I found a note in front of me stating that *Monty Python* had probably won an award and, when I went up to collect it, would I be kind enough to say a few words: I was in no real state to say anything and I could think of very little to say. . . . Panic started to clutch at my vitals as the ceremony started and actor after actress after actperson, feigning surprise, went up to collect their awards on behalf of all the other people who had made all this ('my stardom') possible – e.g. the make-up girls, the hairdressers, the man who cuts the hair of the vet who looks after my poodle etc. Everyone being overwhelmed, overoverwhelmed and even moreoverwhelmed.

The Right Hon. Reginald Maudling was presenting the awards as the cameras poked here and there, picking out 'reaction shots' of sycophantic laughter and synthetic bonhomie.

Suddenly it was my turn – an excerpt from *Monty Python* was shown on a huge screen and I was announced as accepting the award. I left the safety of my table with Colin Welland, Richard Beckinsale and Ray Stevens (accepting an award for Andy Williams) and walked up onto the stage, accepted the oscarine object from Mr Maudling, shook his hand and thanked Mr Murray for the introduction. I then stepped forward to the microphone and, after remarking that I was 'very deeply honoured and would not want to do anything to detract from the dignity of the occasion . . .', let out a howling scream and fell writhing to the floor. Photographers' flashes went off and TV cameras closed in as I crawled all the way down the steps and back to my table on all fours, clutching the award.

The reaction from the guests was startling – some, the sensible ones who had been hoping against hope that something would liven up the ponderous nonsense shrieked with mirth. Ray Stevens heaved a sigh of relief and said, 'Thank God, I've been dying for someone to do that for years . . .' Cilla Black, I noticed, nearly fell off her chair laughing – I've always liked Cilla. Others were shocked. Some thought they ought to be.

Because of the delay in transmission I was able to rush home and watch the entire proceedings two hours later on ITV.

The entire film crew were staying at an hotel in Glencoe, the nearest other human habitation being some twenty-five miles away. We were in festive spirits after a good day's Python filming and there was a skittle alley game in the main bar. Michael Palin and I hit on the idea that the winner of the game should not be the person who'd knocked down the most skittles but the one whose approach with the ball was voted the silliest. Michael picked up the ball, did a couple of pirouettes and dashed out of the hotel, ran round it three times, came in the bar, poured a pint of beer over his head and threw the ball at the scoring board. He was declared the winner without further competition.

I'd noticed a group of climbers who'd settled in one corner near the fire for a few pints after a hard day and so thought I'd join them to exchange a few climbing stories. I knew quite a few of the climbs they were talking about and it became apparent to me that I'd actually led some more difficult climbs myself. I began to talk modestly about these, and then, feeling that I'd been accepted by the group, told them also that I was a 'pouff'. I was pleased that this had no deleterious effect on our companionship and we had several more rounds of raucous drinks. I think they quite enjoyed the anarchic nature of my conversation and I'd noticed that for some time now a young lady dressed in a very 'counties' fashion and obviously quite 'well-to-do-don't-you-know' had been staring in my direction. Eventually she said in quite a commanding tone, 'Why don't you come over here and talk to me?'

I'm not absolutely sure of the details but apparently I climbed onto the table and said, 'Sorry darlin', no luck with me, I'm a pouff.' She left in a huff and the landlord came in in one[1]. I was ejected from the hotel and the doors were bolted on me. I walked around the outside of the hotel, searching for some sort of cover for the night. It was below freezing, sleeting and winding – I couldn't even find a hen-hut or dog-kennel and twenty-five miles would have been a tough proposition.

Eventually the front door opened. Mikey Palin had done some wonderful work on the landlord, explaining that, perhaps I was a touch eccentric, but that I had a heart of gold and I was allowed back inside. We returned to the bar for a nightcap. Now earlier in the day I'd had a moment or two's conversation with the barmaid who'd complained that the landlord had labelled her as a malingerer because she went to hospital in Edinburgh rather too often. I asked about her treatment and examined her neck and thought: 'Mmm. . . . Lymphadenopathy, possibly Lymphadenoma or a blood dyscrasia such as Leukaemia.' Enlarged glands could be felt everywhere. No malingerer she.

Over my nightcap I explained to the landlord the possible nature of the girl's condition about which she presumably had not been told. He was stricken with guilt about having been so hard on her, now realizing that her life-span was likely to be limited and thanked me profusely with more drinks and cigars for Michael and myself.

I'd had so much to drink that evening I just remember climbing into bed, falling out and then being convinced that I had fallen onto the ceiling, where I slept soundly. . . .

1. See note 1 on page 74.

CHAPTER SIXTEEN

A Penultimate Chapter

George Melly did a series of late-night chat shows for Granada TV and his idea was to have guests who were really friends so that there would be no need for a clipboard full of questions prepared by researchers – just George and his guest.

He kindly invited me onto the programme. I remember the pre-show hospitality was particularly lavish and the interview suitably outrageous – I finished up trying to train the audience to play 'Shitties'[1].

Some weeks later a letter arrived at the Python office via the BBC TV Centre. This was from an extremely angry lady who said that someone from *Monty Python* – who had not had the courage to give his name (I didn't need to, George introduced me and there it was in the closing credits), had appeared on the George Melly programme and had admitted to being a homosexual. Her handwriting became visibly angrier as she went on to say that persons like that should not be allowed to live and

1. See page 221.

would suffer eternal torment in the fires of hell and were an abomination. There was much more self-righteous invective, promising more fire and brimstone, followed up by some twenty pages of prayers which if they were repeated by the offender twice daily would at least place him in some kind of purgatory instead.

Eric Idle wrote back to the 'lady', saying that we ('The Pythons') had found out which one it was and killed him. . . .

Curiously enough, we did the next TV series without John Cleese.

I wonder what she thought. . . .

Several years earlier, there was a charity football match. M. Python and some others were playing 'Someone Else'. I didn't want to get involved with actually playing and so I did my charitable bit by turning up as the 'Colonel' and marched up and down the field barking orders – lying in the goal-mouth, just generally making a nuisance of myself. I find football an entirely tedious game anyway.

Someone, I didn't know till then he was called Keith Moon, also thought that the game needed more life and drove a car onto the pitch, grabbed the ball and scored. The game became suitably muddled after that and we all went into the club house for 'drinkies'. Keith and I seemed to have some kind of instant rapport and certainly we both liked drink.

We played an old St Swithin's game called 'Shitties' – in which teams compete in trying to deposit three coins held between the buttocks into a pint pot placed ten feet away from the starting line. . . .

A few more drinks and then back to Keith's place – an amazing construction of plate glass and concrete with octaphonic sound in every room, all playing different tracks, a howling dog and a nearly ex-wife locked in a broom cupboard. . . . Here we had more drinks and apologized for having driven over Keith's chauffeur's hat – he reminisced gleefully about a few recent 'outrages' and outlined a change of policy. Instead of destroying repellent hotel rooms, he had decided on a more constructive approach. Every visitor should smuggle in a suitcase full of building materials, so that he could build some annoyingly permanent memento, like a brick dog kennel, in the middle of the room.

I left at about three or four in the morning, Keith providing me with a bottle of Scotch for the long journey from Chertsey – very considerate – I would have done the same for him and have. The next time I remember meeting Keith was after a concert at the Sundown in Edmonton (London) – amazing . . . the balcony oscillated fully six inches in the middle and the walls could be seen vibrating with the wonderful noise of 'The Who'. . . . I found I could actually understand the words if I put my fingers in my ears. . . .

I went round back stage afterwards to congratulate Keith, 'Great, loved it' etc. I said, 'I could hear some of the words with my fingers in my ears.'

Keith laughed and a diminutive, grey-haired old lady said, 'Shall I hit him Keith or will you?'

Keith said, 'Oh you do it.' She then swiftly lifted one of her little legs and kicked me in the balls. Fortunately she just missed these sensitive parts and I said magnanimously, 'Go on, have another go,' expecting her to give up. But she didn't and clipped the lower bit of my left testicle. 'Waaaarrrggghhh,' I went.

Keith apologized for his mother-in-law's behaviour and suggested we should go for a drink. For once I didn't feel like a drink and left, promising to see him again as soon as I felt better. . . .

The next time I saw Keith was at the Londonderry Hotel – the only hotel in London which would accept him and even then his penthouse suite was registered under the name of 'Rupert Wilde'.

I called at the Londonderry and asked for Mr Wilde's suite – it was on the top floor – the eleventh I think. I arrived to find Keith and a few assorted girls but no gin and tonic – I filled in with a beer or two, while we waited for the gin Keith had immediately ordered from room-service on my arrival.

Fifteen minutes later. Still no sign of G. & T.'s. Keith rang room-service to tell them that if the drinks didn't arrive within the next five minutes their colour TV would arrive on the pavement. Keith became impatient and disappeared out of the window. I realized that this in itself was extraordinary more than ten floors up. I looked out of the window expecting to see a balcony but no – there was no balcony and no Keith, only a four-inch-wide ledge extending round the building. I wouldn't have gone out there but then I wasn't Keith. I sat back and

Keith was never dull

waited, sipping at a beer, then Keith reappeared through the window carrying a bottle of Beefeater gin which he plonked on the table saying, 'There you are, Graham.' He'd made his way along the ledge and broken into the next-door penthouse suite and stolen the bottle from their drinks cabinet.

Keith was never dull – nobody could ever accuse him of that and whenever the two of us arrived together in his old local or my current one, the Angel, there was an air of expectancy; something was about to happen. He was never predictable and arrived at the pub one evening while a quiet charity raffle of a cake and a basket of fruit was in progress for Hornsey Handicapped Children. The unenthusiastic bidding was flagging at £1.50p for the fruit. Keith immediately put in a bid of £45 and startled everyone by paying another £50 for the cake, and the people there who had been expecting trouble at the sight of him had to revise their opinions.

We then went back to my place for a few drinkies and a friend of mine from the pub, Dennis, found a naughty lady of the night and with the aid of Keith's white Rolls-Royce Phantom brought her to the house. At the point where Keith seemed about to eat a butterfly she had tattooed near to her naughty bits, I suddenly decided that it was ice-axe[1] time and that everyone should leave. Keith later correctly ascribed this to jealousy, in that everything would have been fine if a suitable young man had been found as well. . . .

'The Who' were doing three charity Christmas concerts at the Hammersmith Odeon. Keith asked me if I would help out by filling in between acts. 'Yes,' I said. I prepared a little bit of nonsense to perform and had a ridiculous song, 'Yah de Buckety' written out on a sheet to be lowered so that I could get the audience to sing, relieving some of my burden. No-one had come to the theatre to hear my attempts at humour, they wanted 'The Who'. I had a difficult time, gave up in mid-monologue and cut to the end song and got off. Keith said, 'You were lousy and drunk.' I agreed that I'd been lousy but the drunkenness was immaterial. I told him not to worry, now that I'd got the audience 'sussed' I'd have something better worked out for the next two nights. . . .

The next night I arranged for my microphone to be put

1. A mountaineer's primitive way of ejecting unwanted callers.

through the same amplification system as 'The Who', walked out on the stage and asked the audience for ten minutes of abuse. They started shouting a few obscenities. Then, through the full amplification I told them that this was not good enough – 'I meant real abuse – that was rotten, feeble,' I shouted over their now mounting yells of 'Shithead, cunt' etc. I then stood back and looked at my wrist watch encouraging them occasionally, if their abuse showed any signs of waning in intensity. After ten minutes was up I got them to sing the song and everyone was in the right mood for 'The Who.' I came off stage and there was Keith grinning – 'Fucking great,' he said . . . the third night was no problem either. . . .

The most frightening appearance I've ever made was doing a similar job filling in between acts for 'Pink Floyd' at their Knebworth outdoor concert. Walking up onto that stage alone to face 90,000 people was alarming. (I include this as an example of the self-aggrandisement posing as humility common to all autobiographies.)

The film *Monty Python and the Holy Grail* made a lot of money for me (and for me it was a lot). Unfortunately the tax people demanded 83% of this (cf. pineal gland, Chapter 3) but, having a little left, I decided to invest it in something I knew about.

Some years before Bernard McKenna had written a half hour TV play for Ronnie Barker called *The Odd Job*. I liked this and thought that it would form the basis for a very funny film, the idea being that a man who had found himself incapable of committing suicide hires an odd job man to do the job for him. Knowing his own weakness, he tells the man not to take any notice should he appear to change his mind or make any attempt to preserve his life: just bump him off. The odd job man leaves. The central character's reasons for wanting to commit suicide then disappear with the reappearance of a forgiving wife but now there is a man out there with a contract on him whom he has no way of contacting and who would take no notice even if he did. Keith, I thought, would make an excellent Odd Job Man. I commissioned a script from Bernard and the process of film producing began. Eventually I had a script that I was happy with. Keith and I were to play the leads and I'd found sufficient financial backing – about half a million pounds – the production was on.

Now Keith had a problem with alcohol, just as I had, indeed I first began to realize how ill I was becoming having sat at Keith's bedside on the occasions when he was suffering (and I mean suffering) from withdrawal symptoms. He'd hallucinated that he was losing weight to the extent that he would shortly no longer exist and had to keep weighing himself for reassurance. He also thought that the S.A.S. were after him and had him tied to the bed for one entire night with wired electrodes either side of his testicles so that, if he shook, or moved at all the shock would be very nasty indeed. It's difficult to remain motionless when you have D.T.s. This was an horrific experience for him. Two weeks away from shooting Keith was in hospital drying out to get fit, ready for the filming.

Unfortunately the director I had engaged, Cliff Owen, had broken his thigh a week earlier and we now had a new director, Peter Medak. Feeling lucky to find a director who would be willing to take on the task at such short notice, I took Peter to see Keith in hospital where we did a little read-through of a couple of scenes. We left the hospital. Peter Medak became convinced that my best friend was not the right person for the job: I felt he was wrong but there was little I could do about it. My executive producers (they provide a lot of the actual cash) preferred to take Peter's judgement on this issue, despite a vigorous protestation from me directly to Peter's main ally in this, a chap called Steve O'Rourke, manager of 'Pink Floyd', to whom I said that I had only begun to be interested in this project from the start because this was 'exactly the right role for Keith' and that, without him, the film would just become a 'British B. Feature' or worse.

Short of cancelling filming altogether, there was nothing I could do. My co-producers, executive producers and even the author, Bernard, all were expressing doubts as to Keith's ability – in part they were worried, I suppose, about his drinking but, damn it, they were wrong. I knew the two of us would see it through: by this time I had been off alcohol for three months. I had a sleepless night. I knew how much Keith was looking forward to the part in the film: I knew that I was right and they were wrong but should I just wave goodbye to the £50,000 I had already spent or make the film and take a chance on it making money? I chose the latter and still wish I hadn't.

226

Keith was very understanding about it all but I knew how much it must have hurt him.

At the same time EMI had just backed out of their deal with Python about providing $4,000,000 for *The Life of Brian* production. Lord Delfont himself gave us the chop above the heads of the chiefs of EMI production who had agreed the terms. Keith set about vigorously trying to raise the money for us to save this venture and would have succeeded in time. But George Harrison made an extremely courageous offer which was eagerly accepted by us and the film was on again. Keith was going to play the part of one of the blood-and-thunder prophets in that and when I met him a week before we went off to start shooting in Tunisia he seemed to be looking forward to it all very much. He was still not drinking and had, it seemed, beaten the bottle. But on September 7th 1978 he died . . . having drunk a quantity of wine and taken some heminevrin[1] pills, a deadly combination.

I did not know how to react – the loss was too appalling to comprehend but it left me determined to make sure that his spirit – his visions of right and wrong – his energy would not die with him. Keith was kindness itself and never harmed anyone in his escapades, which certainly brightened up many lives – just because there was someone around who was reckless enough to say, 'Stuff the lot of you!' and drive his Rolls-Royce into a swimming pool. Or blow the door off an hotel bedroom with dynamite because a pompous hotel manager complained about his cassette recorder making 'a noise' in the lobby. The amazed manager, staring at the smoking doorway as Keith pointed at his cassette, still playing, was told, 'That's *noise* mate – this is "The Who".' . . . Keith is one person I know I'll see again. . . .

. . . Now, as luck and Capt. W. E. Johns would have it, everything went air force blue with flashes of gold. . . . We hurtled towards the 'safe' pericentre of the black hole of Orion, employing occasional plasma ramjet thrusts to avoid a clutch of indescribable singularities, arriving light years away, but,

1. A drug sometimes used to avert the foulest horrors of alcohol withdrawal (see Chapter o).

David swims past

simultaneously, in Los Angeles two years later.

I had slipped into a state of inertia. All further activity seemed pointless. I had fallen foul of one of my own footnotes.[1] For months now I'd been suffering from this ill-defined mental malaise. Nothing seemed real any more. Was this just the effect of living in Los Angeles, in which case I should leave immediately; or was there some deeper psycho-pathology? I called Dr One Across to examine me. As we sipped our apricot Shastas we chatted amiably about how it was now two years since our encounter in Chapter Nought. He was pleased that I had successfully kicked the habit of twenty-three thirty-sevenths of a lifetime but again gave analytical flummery the elbow and said, 'Do you realize that in the ten minutes I have been here you've dropped seventeen famous names?'

'Have I?' I said. 'I didn't intend to, it's just that I happen to know these people. They're friends of mine . . . er, they live here. . . .'

'I want you to repeat what you've just said to yourself and think about it as a medical man.'

'You mean I've got. . .?'

My head reeled as the grim reality struck me like a blow on the head from a copy of Cecil and Loeb.[2]

'Yes, Nivenism,' he said. 'It's a common enough complication of Angelitis, a similar disease to that described by Freud as the Frank Harris Syndrome, an endemic autobiographical complaint.'

'What should I do, move to Finland?'

'No, you must face the problem. There is no known treatment. You'll just have to sweat it out.'

'Isn't there anything I can do to speed up my recovery?'

'There is, but it isn't going to be pleasant I'm afraid – Revulsion Therapy. I'm going to prescribe for you an intensive course of Hollywood Parties; it's your only hope.'

1. See p. 69, note 2.
2. See p. 80, note 1.

CHAPTER SEVENTEEN

The Mood is a Full Baboon

It was 12.30. A 900081 cc Harley-Davidson-Mitsubushi-Cranston-Thurbid, black leather-bound, steel-studded City of the Angels' bike, 'iron-throated' its way up the pauntly drive of 204 Bristol Avenue South, Brentwood LA Calif.

'Shheeiiiitttt . . .' drawled David. 'That's Peter.'

Being laid back (obligatory in Southern California), I allowed the customary twenty-minute pause to elapse before responding with, ' 'Pon my soul 'tis.' We allowed another twenty minutes of laid-back time to pass before expecting to hear the doorbell.

'Zzz' it clanged. Both parties either side of the door alpha-rhythmed away a further third of an hour. Finally after a series of languid phone-calls we managed to get through to Starlite Emergency Twenty-Four-Hour-Luxury-Door-Opening-Service. We'd used them before; they were a good firm and for a pittance of a thousand dollars a week would arrive within minutes to open anyone's doors. (There was of

230

course a fifty dollars surcharge for not being in the Beverly Hills area but, in addition to their activities with portals, they would remove any unwanted 'single-portion-pizzas-under-one-metre-in-width'.)

David gave them a Mexican gardener as a tip and showed Peter in.

Peter Bromilow, six feet twelve inches of mock-neo-Nazi-garbed S.S. Rough-trade-Chic, strode into the room and politely asked to be shown the cucumbers in a manner reminiscent of Henry Irving at Agincourt:

> Now grit the teeth and whet the microtome,
> If tea party there be let cucumber
> Be sliver'd to the thinnest with precision
> And press'd twixt finest slices of good bread. . . .
> (*Exits left into kitchen . . .*)

Starfeest 24-Hour Caterpersons were not to be allowed to interfere with their grotesque Californian ways in the preparation on this most English of occasions. . . . The therapy was under way.

In the kitchen bread was already being thinly sliced with the sharpest of knives dipped in 211° Fahrenheitest water[1] by Duitch Helmer, a Russian Jewish Princess and session-singing-side-saddle-riding veterinarian's assistant, while in another corner of the room a grinning, momentarily apostate tunesmith son of Cyd Charisse was mixing some 'Elixir Grimsdaecii'; its influence pervading the very atmosphere. . . .__

'Zzzzz,' rustled the doorbell, heralding the arrival and swift Starlite-assisted admittance of Barbara and Dr Timothy Leary. The blissful couple appeared to have attained 'Glitnir', 'Yima's vara', call it what you will[2]; but they had definitely uncoiled Kundalini right up past their sahasrāras. They had eschewed years of meditation in a lotus posture, tedious attempts at withdrawing attention from perceptual cognitions, and weeks of leafing through back-numbers of *Self Realisation Magazine* and had achieved the same elysian state

1. A tip I once picked up from an Archbishop of Canterbury.
2. I like 'Mahasamadhi'. (D.)[3]
3. Mm, I'll think about it . . . Aum . . . Aum . . . Aum. (G.)

231

by the use of chemical additives. As the couple glid past, Timothy's blue-grey eyes gazed with radium-like lustre into something that might as well be described as Eternity. Their three children, seeing something they wanted in the garden, stampeded earthily over the grand piano, through a token bevy of uninvited journalists, across the lawn, leapt over the recumbent naked form of a friend of David Hockney and straight into the pool fully clothed.

'Isn't that George Lazenby over there, seen enjoying a can of specially imported Foster's Lager?'

'What, you mean behind Christopher Isherwood and Georgia Brown seen there enjoying a joke with Ian le Fresnais?' queried the second token-journalist.

'Yes, between Peter Cook, Dudley Moore, Bo Diddley and the piano, seen over there enjoying a brief rest in a tight schedule. Who's that with Hollywood psychiatrist Dr Stuart Lerner?'

'It could be either Jane Seymour, Jenny Agutter, Susan George, Shelley Duvall or Victor Borge.'

'Victor Borge?'

'Sorry, did I say Victor Borge? Only I also thought I caught sight of Victor Borge enjoying a quiet word with Charlton "Chuck" Heston and screen-writer-companion, Alan Katz. . . .'

'Yes, but who's the girl with Stuart Lerner?'

'Oh that's Sylvia Kristel.'

'Oh. . . .'

The sun dappled its way through the trees, spilling onto the crisp white linen of the tea table which ran the full length of the garden. Cucumber sandwiches were passed. Tea was poured from silver pots into bone china and the soft 'Clop' of croquet mallet hitting ball wafted across the lawn. . . . A token-journalist four yards away thought that the party was in full swing and I could hear the distant drone of Bernard McKenna throwing up after his second bottle of Bourbon. Thank heavens we'd given him his own quarters. 'Everyone seems to be occupied,' I thought as I slipped through the guests, nodded to Burt Reynolds' chauffeur and stepped discreetly through a side-door and into a waiting presidential limo. Now for phase two. . . .

It was coincidentally David Frost's fortieth birthday party, his third that afternoon, and I'd promised to try and look in for a moment or two. I'm glad I did, for there in the main ballroom, seated at the top table, completely surrounded by journalists, was David Paradine Frost. David was so preoccupied that he was unaware that table upon table of celebrities to grace this magnificent occasion had sent along cardboard cutouts of themselves. There sat an effigy of Peter Sellers; at another table a photograph of James Coburn chatted to an image of Dick Van Dyke: between them one could see the outline of Andy Williams standing in for a silhouette of Ray Stevens. Mary Tyler-Moore, Jane Fonda, Gabe Caplan, Victor Borge and David Niven had arrived as a group shot. David thanked a two-dimensional Henry Kissinger for his thoughtful gift of two dozen fresh sycophants and even more effusively thanked one of his secretaries for having had the absolutely superbly fantastic and original idea of inviting his mother along. Then, almost as if on cue, a singing telegram arrived: a refugee from a Busby Berkeley musical mawked her way through a cloying paean of praise for David's unique achievement. This was followed by a dancing telegram, followed by a dancing-and-singing telegram, then a dancing-singing telegram on roller skates dressed like a birthday cake. David even managed to feign surprise when a fifth telegram, a roller-skating-shouting-singing comedy duo arrived. For once, David had made a slight miscalculation. Even his synthesized smile showed signs of sagging, fortunately perking up professionally for each photographic flash.

Luckily Peter Sellers' cardboard cutout had lost interest in the proceedings and I was able to make my exit hiding behind it as it excused itself on grounds of ill health; it'd apparently been bitten on the shin by a tiger whilst skiing. . . .

On the way out I consoled an agitated Rod Stewart, who'd unfortunately had to come to the party in person. He had only got married that morning and the blow-ups of the happy couple could not be processed in time.

A Carmen Mirandatal host-person with eerily nude legs assisted me to my seat on the Star-Minder-Sit-'Em-Easy-Limo-Loader. As I was glidden hydraulically to my seat in the presidential limo, through the darkened glass I caught a

His third that afternoon

234

glimpse of Peter's cutout being loaded with intensive care into a Rolls-Royce Silver Cloud Phantambulance. I pressed the audio 'off' switch on the colour TV and settled back to listen to D. Bowie's 'Kooks' on the car's septemphonic sound system, took a can of diet loganberry Shasta from the bar, and sipped at it in between puffs on a j. of Antarctic Beige, nibbling sporadically from a plastic bag full of mushrooms.

As we fluoresced our way westward along Sunset, past a shimmering Château Marmont, another limo glowed along-side. Its sun-roof slid back and a figure stood up to wave cheerily at some ladies with long legs standing outside the Body Shop. It was Eric Idle. I pressed the 'raise' button on my arm-rest and went up to the sun-deck position. Eric had disappeared inside. I told the driver to get me his number and picked up the handset. Seconds later I heard the phone ring in the next-door car. After the usual pleasantries of 'Hello Eric,' 'Hello Graham, what are you on?' had been exchanged, he, Ricky F'Tang and Penelope Elm crossed over on their limo-loader.

'Would you all like to come to a party at my place later on?' I asked, as I passed round a brown paper bag filled with cookies and poured them large vodkas on the rocks.

'I think we're already at one,' replied Eric.

'George said he'd try to drop by and I know Harry and Richard are going to be there later.'

'All right, see you later,' said Eric. 'It's OK if we bring Keith and Ron isn't it?'

'Sure – OK see you later, I'm just going to nip off down through "Boystown" on the way back – I want to pick up some "Zoom" . . .'

'I bet that's not all. . . .' twinkled Eric.

It was dark as I and a few guests I'd found en route at a party in the Polo Lounge arrived back at 203 Bristol Ave., North. A young Texan, an Irish choirboy and a Thai busboy called 'Bum', were not among them. Van Dyke Parkes greeted me with, 'We all *love* your style, Graham, and to me that's as important as ducks in June.' I agreed wholeheartedly and went into the main room. . . .

It must have been something I'd eaten; the house seemed

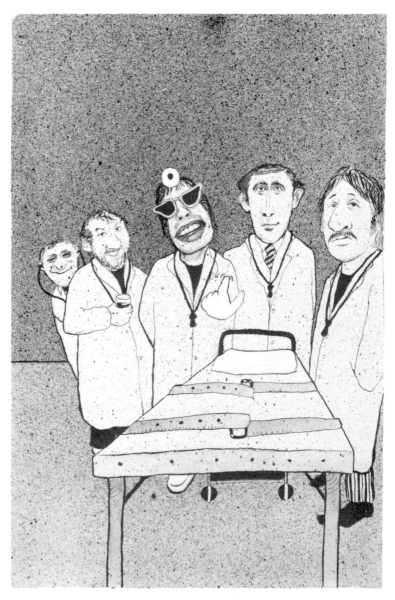

I stared at people, hoping that they wouldn't notice how strange they looked to me.

236

to be full of an assemblage of images, sounds and smells and other sensations, mediated through a spot two inches behind the nape of my neck and all the way up the inside of my trousers. I stared at people, hoping that they wouldn't notice how strange they looked to me: normally this did not bother me. I'd probably been smoking too much. . . .

Harry Nilsson was at the piano performing a duet with a barking robot-dog. Ringo then led a rendition of 'Happy Birthday to You' accompanied by twenty-five lead vocalists who just happened to be there and countless session singers, a gift from Warner Bros. Harry and Marty Feldman added a touch of Keith Moon by using the top of the piano as a drum kit. My mother and father hovered in a state of enlightened astonishment at having found yet another black man who was 'Very well spoken, you know'. . . .

Taking a cue from Marty, who was by now chasing Hollywood-psychiatrist Stuart Lerner around the room, trying to embarrass him with a French kiss, I chatted up the nearest sex symbol, Sylvia Kristel, telling her to pop in and see Bernard McKenna, who I felt needed a sexual threat to slow down his rapidly developing affair with a gallon of Bourbon. She returned a few moments later, her advances having been repelled by an inflight ashtray. She wandered off into the garden to be consoled by a girlfriend.

Tony Stratton-Smith, First Earl of Lambourn-Elect, schoonered past beatifically murmuring mantrillically, 'Ah Brazil, Ah Brazil, Ah Brazil . . .' George Harrison, an island of purity, glowed nearby with a 'Hello Graham,' and a self-realization-fellowship-wave. My mother didn't think that Ron Woods and Keith Richards should have been allowed into my bedroom since they were Eric's guests and she was very worried about whether 'those two girls were all right out there in the bushes'. . . . I let her worry away happily . . . Loretta Feldman told a bemused Eric how full of shit[1] people could be in an explanatory bellow, Elton John appeared without his cap and spectacles, a bubbling liberated pauntly soul. . . .

Image followed image until early morning: the house was

1. Californian banter.

almost empty but the drumming at the piano had resumed and continued until near dawn when Marty and Loretta left, leaving Harry, who couldn't understand people's lack of stamina and called me a shit as I saw him firmly to his limo – 'Yes, I am,' seemed the appropriate reply. Out there at 6.30 am he screamed at the top of his voice in the direction of Hollywood, exclaiming that it, too, was full of shit. I bellowed in agreement with my friend, as his limo 'thhffed' off down the drive towards the rising sun. Dr One Across gave me a conspiratorial thumbs-up from the bushes.

Thankfully I closed the door and Star-tu-bed, Tuckers-in-to-the-Stars (No-Kids-or-Animals!) saw me to bed, not forgetting to clean my teeth. . . . I fell asleep as a girl with brown knees finished chapter nine of *Biggles Grits His Thighs*. . . .

'The moon,' yawned Algy opiningly, 'is rather a dull place,' and all of us decided that we would definitely leave the following Tuesday.

Even at 1/6 G the pogo-sticks had become a bore. The daily round of long-distance TV chat shows, panel-games about extra-terrestrial things, guest-appearances on *This Is Your Planet*, all of which conveniently defy description, became about as interesting as breakfast at Tiffany's. It was Sunday afternoon and the pubs were all shut. After half an hour of sexual reminiscences about things that none of us had ever done, we decided to have a farewell party. . . . David made the cucumber sandwiches, John prepared James Grims-dyke's famous punch, and I slipped out in my beige space-suit to see if any of the others would be prepared to pop along.

The Beast and Anna Karenina were doing the hoovering, John Cleese's diary was absolutely chock-a-block, and Nostradamus had left a note on the door of his capsule saying, 'I predict I'll be back about eight.'

I was about to give up, but thought, without much hope, 'I may as well call in on the Alis.' Mrs Ali was regurgitating masticated carrots into the champ's mouth as he was being rubbed down by his old space-partner.

'Can you come to our party?' I asked.

'Man, I'd love to,' he said. 'But no, I can't.'

'I'm sorry about that,' I said. 'But why not?'

'Look, I've spent twelve years building up the reputation of being a loud-mouthed buck-nigger. Do you want me to spoil that by coming round to your place and being as intelligent as I really am?'

'Yes, I suppose that would blow your cover a bit, old man,' I said.

'You bet, man.'

I stepped out nimbly through the airlock and deftly percolated past Elton John's piano-shaped moon-buggy. He was obviously entertaining David Bowie and Ken Liberace, so I passed on. I knew the next space-vehicle was occupied for an 'at home' evening by David Hockney and Alan Bennett comparing the size of their accents, so I didn't bother with them. I then molested my way past J. B. Priestley, HRH The Queen Mother, David Niven (please note), Peter Sellers, Britt Ekland, Carlo Ponti, Peter Cook and Bo Dudley, 'a' but not 'the' Dr Jonathan Miller, HRH The Very Dead Governor of New Zealand, Noel Coward, George Melly, and Larry and Gerry Durrell. Unfortunately they all had 'slight chills' that evening.

Keith Moon, Richard Starkey, and Harry Nilsson were genuinely disappointed that they couldn't come, in that they weren't in the lunar regions at the time, but wished us all well.

In desperation I knocked on the hatch of a capsule made entirely of wood. There was no reply. I undid the mahogany latch on the huge teak door and approached the coffin. Engraved in the oak were the words, 'Here lies Oscar Fingal O'Flaherty Wilde, gone out for good.' I'd had enough excuses for one day. I wrenched open the Lombardy poplar lid with a noise resembling a loud rustle, which means nothing on earth but in outer space can often even split your nose. I took hold of the dead wit's legs and dragged him back to my place.

'There is a time in the affair of grebes, which, taken at the cludge, leads on to brutalness. A man is not a wasp, not Düsseldorf built in a day. Damon Runyon had a bunyon, and for a' they say hae' I. My heart bakes, a drowsy numbness fills my Jenssen, let it be, let it be.'

'What's that supposed to mean?' asked David.

'It's not bad. He *is* dead!' I said.

'Oh come on "he is dead. It's not bad!" '

'No come on, Wilde, what does that mean?' asked the Prince of Wales.

'It means, Your Majesty . . . it means. . . .'

The audience exploded into laughter.

We all ran offstage, and John Cleese hissed angrily into my ear, 'Learn your fucking lines. It should have been . . .

You had us waiting for hours.'

GRAHAM (*faintly*): I didn't think anyone noticed.

JOHN (*even more faintly*): No, I suppose they didn't.

GRAHAM (*and still more faintly*):

THE END